Adornments

Myra Callan

Photography by Elizabeth Messina

NORTH LIGHT BOOKS

CINCINNATI, OHIO

Dedication

For my parents, Jung and Hwa; loving husband, Matt; one and only sister, Amy; and grandmother, Ok Boon.

CONTENTS

INTRODUCTION 6

CHAPTER ONE
MATERIALS, TOOLS AND TECHNIQUES   8
  MATERIALS   10
  TOOLS   16
  TECHNIQUES   20

CHAPTER TWO
FLOWERS   28
  GOLDEN FLORAL WRIST CORSAGE   30
  BLUSHING SILK PETALS HAIR COMB   36
  PATTERNED SILK FLOWERED HEADBAND   42
  PETITE SILK CLUSTER FLOWER COMB   48
  BLOSSOM AND PEARL COMB   52
  BLOSSOM AND PEARL NECKLACE   58
  OVERSIZED HANDMADE SILK FLOWER COMB   64

CHAPTER THREE
FEATHERS   68
  FEATHER SPRAY BROOCH   70
  FEATHER AND BURNT SILK PETAL HAIR CLIP 74
  SOFT FEATHER DANGLE EARRINGS   80
  PINK CURVED FEATHER NECKLACE   86
  LACE EMBELLISHED BOBBY PIN   92

CHAPTER FOUR
FLOURISHES   96
  SOFT PETAL AND APPLIQUÉ NECKLACE   98
  LACE POUF BLOSSOM BROOCH   106
  DOUBLE-FINISHED LACE FLOWER NECKLACE   110
  CREAMY LACE BELT   116
  LACE AND LEAF HEADBAND   120
  SILVER ROSETTE MINI HAT   124
  SILK BLOSSOM DANGLE EARRINGS   128
  DUSTY GREEN AND GRAY SILK FLOWER
  AND LACE BELT   134

RESOURCES   140
INDEX   141
ABOUT THE AUTHOR   142

INTRODUCTION

After I started my own business of creating adornments, Twigs & Honey, my mother asked me where I learned the techniques and how I came up with my designs. I told her that I originally learned from her. When I was little, I would watch my mom sew skirts together and arrange flowers for weddings and church services. She never received formal training and didn't use patterns. I would collect the scraps from her projects and create my own accessories and dolls. I had an active imagination. If I couldn't find a particular toy I desired, I would make it myself. My father also created anything I needed that involved wood, and he was meticulous about drawing plans and measuring materials. He made bird houses and wooden homes for my pet mice and built ponds and a multi-level deck in our backyard. While my mother had a keen sense for style and balance, my father had the ability to build with tools and precision. I think I adopted an equal mix of characteristics from both my mother and father, and in doing so, developed a unique skill set and solid foundation for design.

By junior high, I loved to create, but it was just a hobby. I decided to focus on my studies, which later resulted in a degree in geography with a focus on environmental science. I was a perfectionist and didn't feel confident that my hobbies could sustain the livelihood I envisioned, so I planned on becoming a scientist researching environmental change. After working for the government for over a year, I yearned to create beautiful things. The perfect opportunity presented itself while planning my wedding. With a shoestring budget, I decided to make hair accessories for my bridesmaids and myself so I could create exactly what I wanted within a realistic budget. The wedding was beautiful, and I married the love of my life on September 8, 2007. Everything was going well, but after returning from our honeymoon, I felt unfulfilled by my current career path. In January 2008, I listed my first hair accessory, a feathery flower, on Etsy. Within a week, I had sold the one piece in my shop and started receiving custom order requests. My little business took off, and

I put in my notice at work just two months later when I realized I was putting more than full-time hours into my creative business. As frightening as it was to leave a secure income, I was excited to be able to create for a living.

Twigs & Honey has grown in leaps and bounds since its modest beginnings, and it has provided me with an outlet that is more fulfilling than any other occupation I could have imagined for myself. Through the business, I've rediscovered my love for creating. The pieces I enjoy making are a mixture of multiple fashion styles and categories. It's freeing to be able to create such a variety of pieces and to source all manner of materials. Experimentation is such a wonderful thing.

This book is a collection of projects that utilize an assortment of supplies and techniques. You'll learn how to create flowers by hand, curl feathers and incorporate lace. The projects showcase some of my favorite materials and most-loved styles. The book demonstrates the methods, but the possibilities are nearly limitless in terms of end results, as you'll be able to use your own found and treasured components. From vintage millinery flowers to freshwater pearls, you can adjust the projects to reflect your own personal sense of style. With some easy-to-learn skills, you'll be able to create beautiful adornments that are suitable for any occasion.

My mom still helps me with some of my design projects, and I still ask my dad basic questions about construction and building. I think that you never truly stop learning and growing. I'm constantly trying to broaden my skill set and learn something new. Have fun making these projects and creating them with friends and family. Try your own variations by hunting down lovely accent fabrics and delicate bits. I hope you enjoy creating these projects as much as I enjoyed designing and developing them.

Myra Callan

CHAPTER ONE

Materials, Tools and Techniques

IN THIS CHAPTER, you will develop a useful set of skills that will help you create any of the projects in this book. You will learn how to press petals to create handmade flowers and how to hand-sew embellishments. You will also learn common jewelry-making techniques, including wire wrapping and beading. These basic skills will lay the path for creating and designing your own unique pieces.

Keep in mind that you don't have to use the exact same materials listed in the individual projects. You can use colors and fabrics of your choice. This allows you to use those scraps of fabric you've collected through the years and the vintage beads you may have found at a flea market. Have fun and experiment to create pieces that you'll love to make and wear.

MATERIALS

I LIKE TO COLLECT all kinds of beautiful materials, including a variety of feathers, laces and fabrics. I find special fabrics both in stores and online. I have found many laces and embellishments at antique shops and online auction websites. I will often purchase something not because I have a particular project in mind, but because I like it and know I'll find the perfect piece to use it for at some point. Finding amazing materials is always fun. Keep your eyes open and look in many different places to find fabrics and lovely bits you can incorporate into projects.

Beads

I use a variety of beads for my projects, including seed beads, pearls, crystals, rhinestones and semiprecious stone beads. All these beads vary in price, so use the bead that fits your budget and project. Rhinestones and crystals tend to be more costly but can be worth the investment, as they are high impact. Pearls can range in prices, but some freshwater pearls are amazingly affordable. You can also find faux pearls that look very close to the real thing but are lower in cost.

Fabric Flowers

Using manufactured fabric flowers in your pieces is a wonderful timesaver and can also result in truly beautiful finished pieces. The quality and appearance of these flowers varies greatly, as does the materials they are made from. Fabric flowers are most commonly made from cotton, silk, velvet and polyester blends. You can find more affordable fabric flowers at major craft stores. I also like to purchase flowers on millinery, craft, floral and vintage websites. I've built a large collection of lovely fabric flowers through the years, and it's nice to be able to pull from my selection as needed. Some fabric flowers can be quite expensive or difficult to find. It might be beneficial to find a few online millinery stores using a search engine and purchase a variety of sizes and colors.

Feathers

Feathers add a bit of softness or drama to a piece. Most major craft stores carry a selection of feathers. If you can't find the colors or varieties you like, try looking online, as there are numerous websites that sell a large variety of feathers in almost every color imaginable. I sometimes find naturally-shed feathers at farmers markets as well. I like to use goose, rooster and ostrich feathers. Guinea hen feathers are bold and lovely, and duck, pheasant and peacock feathers are also wonderful to use in projects. Feathers can be curled, bent or stripped. Look for colors that will add something extra special to your pieces.

Leaves

Leaf accents work beautifully in accessories. Some fabric leaves look very realistic. Most major craft stores carry an assortment of both fabric flowers and leaf stems. I particularly like using faux dusty miller leaves. These normally come on a branch with several leaf sizes that you can remove to use individually. I also like velvet millinery leaves. You can find both vintage and vintage reproduction velvet leaves online at millinery supply websites and some floral supply websites. I often find great vintage leaves at online auction sites that I save for special pieces. If you can, try to find leaves that are wired, as these are bendable and easy to work with. If you cannot find wired leaves, you can use any artificial leaf and hand-stitch it onto your project. Many fabric flowers come with attached leaves that are usable in accessory projects.

Stamens

Stamens are great for creating realistic fabric flowers or flowers with interesting details in the centers. They come in single loose pieces or in a bunch with a wire stem. I like the stamen bunches for ease, but the loose stamens tend to be easier to find. You can often find these at craft or floral stores, but also try online millinery, craft and cake decorating websites.

Fabric and Felt

You can use a range of different fabric colors, types and textures for the projects in this book. Even patterned fabric can be used to create beautiful and unique flowers. I like to purchase pretty remnants at the craft store, as I usually don't need much and remnants are often sold at a considerable discount. I also like to purchase fabrics at antique shops and online. For a single accessory project, you can often get away with purchasing just ⅛–¼ yard (0.1m–0.2m) of a specific fabric. Use fabrics that are available and accessible to you. When creating pressed flowers, use silk or cotton. Many synthetic fabrics cannot take the high heat required to press the petals and will often burn or even melt. Sometimes you'll find that they can tolerate the heat but won't hold their shape once cooled. When using silk, I like to use silk habotai because it is affordable, dyes easily, comes in a range of thicknesses and is easy to work with. For cottons, I like cotton voile and cotton linen. Cotton is also affordable and easy to dye. You can experiment with other materials, such as silk chiffon and lingerie lace.

You will also use a few types of felt and interfacing or stabilizer. These materials are used as backings to create clean finishes on the backs of pieces and as foundations for belts. It is a good idea to use a dense and flexible felt for finishing pieces and a stiffer felt or interfacing as a foundation material, which will help support embellishments and flowers.

Ribbons

There are so many options for ribbon. They come in many materials and colors and vary in quality. Don't limit yourself to just one type. Ribbons come in very skinny to very wide widths and are perfect for using in self-tie belts, headbands and necklaces. Some styles that work well for the projects in this book include silk, velvet and satin ribbon in ¼"–1½" (6mm–4cm) widths.

Lace Fabric and Lace Appliqués

Lace is a beautiful material to use when embellishing handmade accessories. You can purchase both lace fabric and lace appliqués. Lace fabric can be carefully cut to release the appliqués.

Adhesives and Starches

For the projects in this book, you'll need a good fabric glue and a glue for metals (epoxy). A good fabric glue should be a bit tacky and should dry quickly and clear. Do not attempt to use fabric glue when gluing materials onto metal, as it will likely chip off. Epoxy glue can be toxic, so use it in a well-ventilated space. Most epoxy glues will also need to cure overnight, so plan ahead.

For pressing flower petals, the fabric will need to be prepared using either starch or a fabric stiffener. I like to specifically use fabric stiffeners for flower pressing, and you can find these with adhesives in craft stores. Spray starches work well for stiffening delicate lace and other fabrics. However, you can try both starch and fabric stiffeners and use your favorite.

Alternatively, you can make your own fabric stiffener at home. Place 16 fluid ounces (473ml) in a stainless steel pot and bring to a boil. In a separate glass, mix 1 tablespoon (15ml) of cornstarch with ½ cup (118ml) of water. Slowly add this water and cornstarch mixture into the boiling water and stir until it becomes an almost clear but slightly milky color. Remove the mixture from the heat, add 2 teaspoons (10ml) of white, nontoxic craft glue and mix until completely combined. Once this mixture has cooled, you can use it as a fabric stiffener. Increase or decrease the ingredients as necessary. More glue will create a stiffer fabric, and less cornstarch and glue will create a softer fabric.

Wire, Chain and Findings

For many of the projects, you'll need one or a combination of materials, including wire, chain and jewelry findings. You can use craft, brass, or silver- or gold-colored shaping wire. Depending on your budget, you may also opt to use gold-filled or gold-plated wire. I recommend 28-gauge wire for beading and simpler wire work that uses beads with small holes. Thicker gauge wires are not as easy to work with but are stronger. You can use a variety of thicknesses as needed. You'll also need cloth-covered floral wire. You can normally find this in the floral department of a craft store, and it often comes in white, green or brown. White tends to be best for the projects in this book.

I like to use brass chain because it is economical and has a vintage look. Chains with links that are 2mm to 3mm wide and long tend to work well for the projects in this book, but you may prefer the look of a smaller or larger chain.

Findings needed for the projects in this book include jump rings of various sizes, earring ear wires, eye pins and lobster clasp closures.

Headbands, Clips and Combs

To be able to wear some styles in your hair, you will need the appropriate attachment. This book uses headbands, alligator clips, combs and bobby pins. Satin-covered headbands are great because you can wire, glue or hand sew materials to them. Alligator clips and bobby pins are easy to wear and are affordable. Wire combs are preferable, but you can also choose plastic combs if wire combs are not available. You can also adapt most styles in this book to accommodate a different backing than what is recommended. For instance, if you prefer to wear a headband instead of a comb, you can simply wire or sew the embellishment onto a headband instead.

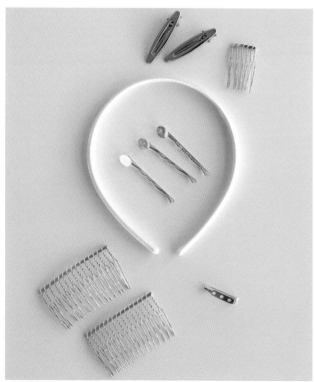

Difficult to Find Materials

Just a quick note on some specific materials you will see in this book: Don't worry about finding a duplicate silk flower or piece of lace for your project. Finding the exact same materials can be challenging, if not impossible. Be open to exploring when shopping for fabric flowers and other materials. Purchase a variety of colors so that you have them at your disposal. For buckram or sinamay hat bases, look online at millinery stores, which often carry a large variety of colors, shapes and sizes.

TOOLS

IN THIS SECTION, you will find all the tools needed to create the projects in this book. Most items are very easy to find at your local craft store. Other tools, like the millinery flower irons, may take a little more time to locate, but, when applicable, alternates are listed for those tools you may have difficulty finding. This section will also discuss the purpose of the tool as it applies to the projects you will be learning.

Millinery Flower Irons

Millinery flower irons are specially made tools for pressing shapes into flat fabric to create dimension and depth. These tools are often made out of solid brass or steel. The irons either come preset into individual wooden handles or as individual tips or attachments. The irons that come attached with wooden handles will require a separate heating source, such as a hot plate or the heating element of a stove top. If the irons are separate attachments, they will require a soldering iron or specially made heating iron. I prefer the attachment style, as it is more portable and supplies consistent, constant heat to the iron attachment. This version can be a harder tool to find, but if you use a common search engine on the Internet, you'll be able to find several online stores that carry these handy tools. You can also find smaller versions at craft and fabric stores, often among needle and quilting supplies. Some sets can be more costly, so it is also beneficial to try and find vintage sets on specialty online collector websites and auction websites.

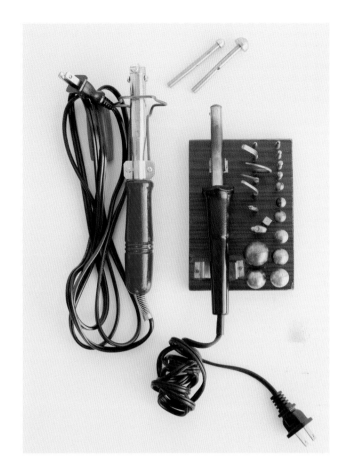

Alternatively, you can use other tools or common household items to press your petals. One alternative is a dapping set. Dapping sets are often used by jewelers to shape metal. You can use them in a similar way to a millinery iron by heating the selected dome with a hot plate and gripping it with a fire-resistant pair of thick gloves or with forceps and an oven mitt. Another option would be to use metal spoons. You can heat up a spoon on a hot plate and grip it with an oven mitt. Experiment with different sizes of spoons until you get the desired result.

For any of the flower-pressing methods, use extreme caution, as high heat can result in accidental fires or burns. Always unplug your tools when they are not in use, and do not leave them unattended. Even after use, ensure that the tools are monitored during cooling, as they can retain very hot temperatures for a considerable amount of time. Keep these items out of reach of small children and pets. Pull long hair back and wear natural fibers. Do not pick up heated tools with your bare hands and do not touch the rod of the soldering or millinery iron, as it can be hotter than the attachment.

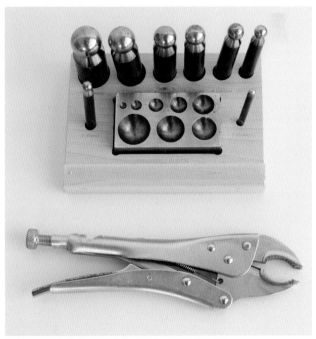

Covered Foam Rubber

When pressing petals, you will need an easy-to-depress pad to help coax the fabric into the desired shape. You can purchase foam rubber from ½"–2" (1cm–5cm) thick. You may want to buy a couple sizes to achieve different results. Cover your foam pad with cotton fabric. Do not use a synthetic fabric, as the high temperatures of the millinery iron will likely burn and melt it.

Sewing Needle and Thread

Most of the projects in this book will require a sewing needle and thread. I like to use sewing needles in a variety of lengths and widths for different tasks. Appliqué needles are good for sewing on tiny beads and freshwater pearls that have smaller holes. When gathering fabric, a longer needle will speed the process. Make sure that you have extra needles, as they can break during use. Also be sure to have needles that will fit through the holes of the beads you are using. You can use any appropriate colored thread, but I personally like to invest in higher quality threads, as I find that with hand-sewn projects they snag and break less.

Scissors

A good pair of scissors can truly do wonders for you. Invest in a high-quality pair of sharp scissors made specifically for cutting fabric. You can choose a length that you feel comfortable using. You may only want to invest in one good pair, as they can be costly, but with time, you might find that having both a long and short pair of sharp scissors is very useful. Large scissors, such as dressmaker scissors, take practice to maneuver when cutting delicate petals, but as you become a better cutter, you'll find that it speeds cutting time significantly. In addition, with practice, using larger scissors minimizes jagged and rough edges. Smaller scissors, such as embroidery scissors, are great for detail work and are a good choice for a novice cutter. They work well for cutting lace appliqués, trimming thread and poking holes in fabric.

I also like to have a couple pairs of cheaper craft scissors that are easily replaceable. I use craft scissors to cut paper, feathers and thicker or rougher materials. Never use your nice fabric scissors to cut anything but fabric. To extend the life of your fabric scissors, do not cut wire, feathers or paper with them; this will quickly dull the blade. From time

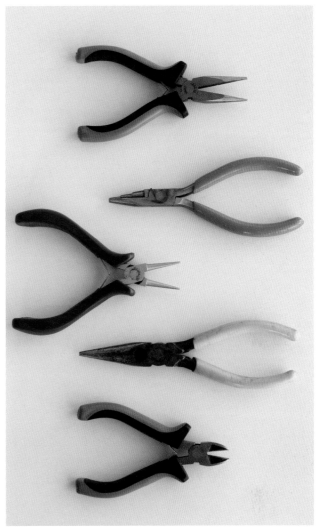

to time, have your fabric scissors sharpened by a professional for a like-new edge. If you accidentally ruin your nice scissors by cutting wire or other rough materials, you can use those as your craft scissors. Through carelessness, I accidentally chipped my first pair of high-quality scissors on a wire, and they've become my go-to pair for cutting feathers for years.

In my toolbox, I keep two pairs of dressmaker scissors, two small embroidery scissors, one pair of pinking shears, one rotary cutter, one pair of paper scissors and several craft scissors. You certainly are not required to have such an extensive assortment, but a variety of scissors can definitely make certain tasks easier and faster.

Jewelry Making Hand Tools

You will need several types of pliers to complete the projects in this book. Chain-nose pliers help grip small findings and get into hard-to-reach places where your fingers may not fit. They are also used to open and close jump rings. You should have two pairs of chain-nose pliers. Round-nose pliers are great for creating curves and loops in jewelry wire. You'll also want a pair of half-round pliers. These look similar to round-nose pliers, but one tip has three different sizes to create three different loop sizes. These pliers also help when wire wrapping is needed to finish a loop. In addition to wires, you will want to have at least one pair of wire cutters for cutting both wire and chain.

TECHNIQUES

SEVERAL TECHNIQUES ARE USED multiple times throughout this book, and they are all simple to learn and require only basic supplies and tools. Through these step-by-step techniques, you will learn how to prepare your fabric, create stamens and work with wire and jewelry findings.

Starching Fabric

In order for your fabric to hold its shape after pressing, it will need to be starched or stiffened so it has a slightly stiff body. Starching will also help prevent fraying and will make cutting shapes much easier. Whether you are using a starch or fabric stiffener, read the directions on the package for specific usage. Most common fabric stiffeners are water soluble, so you can add water to create a more diluted solution, which in turn results in a less-stiff fabric. Depending on the final application, you may want a stiffer or softer fabric. After your fabric has been treated and is wet, hang it to dry. You'll want it to dry as straight as possible and may want to pin down the bottom of the fabric as well. Alternatively, you can dry it flat on a cookie sheet or other laminate surface. If you made your own fabric stiffener as described on page 13, you can either paint on the liquid stiffener or submerge your fabric in the solution and wring out the excess liquid before hanging it or laying it flat to dry.

Shaping and Pressing Petals

Pressing your petals will create a handmade flower that has depth and character. It will turn flat fabric into beautifully shaped fabric. You will use a millinery iron (or other tool as discussed on page 17) to press starched fabric on a foam pad.

YOU WILL NEED

starched fabric

millinery iron with a round ball

heating source (hot plate or soldering iron)

foam rubber pad covered with cotton fabric

scissors

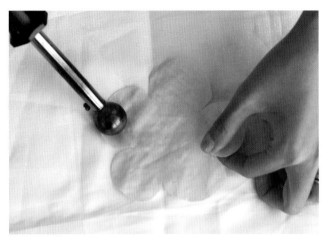

1 Using the iron, press the outer edge of one of the petals. Pressing lightly will create a soft curve in the petal, while pressing more firmly will create a deeper curve. Keep the angle of the iron at about 45 degrees. A shallower angle will require pressing harder to get the same result and can tire your hand and wrist quickly.

2 Continue pressing the outer edge of each petal until all the petal edges have been pressed with the iron.

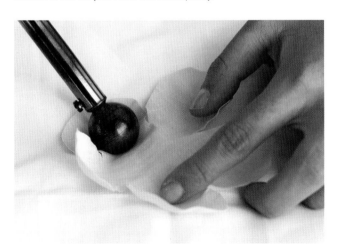

3 Using the iron, press the center of each petal using a slightly circular motion. You can iron over the same parts a few times in order to create a smooth, concave shape.

4 Repeat Step 3 until all petals are fully pressed. You can practice making some layers more or less curved. I like to make the uppermost or smaller layers slightly more pressed than the lower or largest layer. This helps the petals look more separated and the flower look fuller.

Cutting Appliqués From Lace

Lace appliqués can be purchased ready to use, but you can also purchase lace fabric by the yard and hand-cut the appliqués. This can be handy if you find a beautiful bolt of lace at the fabric store. You can purchase ⅛–¼ of a yard (0.1m–0.2m) and cut out several usable appliqués. Other times, you may find a small remnant of vintage lace. By cutting out the appliqués, you'll be able to use the lace even though there is only a small amount.

YOU WILL NEED

lace fabric with clearly defined appliqués

scissors

1 Lace appliqués are typically sewn into tulle. Cut into the tulle and between the lace appliqués unless you have to cut through some lace due to the design.

2 Loosely cut out an appliqué to separate it from the rest of the fabric.

3 Begin cutting more closely around the lace appliqué pattern. Cut closely to, but not directly into, the lace appliqué. Cutting too closely may separate the actual lace cording from the tulle it has been sewn into. Leave about ⅛" (3mm) of tulle around the lace appliqué.

4 Once the piece has been fully cut, it's ready to use on many different types of projects, from an embellishment on a cardigan to an accent on a headband or belt.

Making Stamen Clusters

Creating a cluster or bunch of stamens is pretty easy and straightforward. You may want to make a batch of these at once for ease. Making your own clusters is useful, as the premade bunches are becoming more difficult to source.

YOU WILL NEED

floral tape

cloth-covered floral wire

7–12 or more individual double-sided stamens

scissors

wire cutters

1 Align the individual stamens so they are even. Bend or fold them in half.

2 Insert the cloth-covered floral wire through the bend in the stamens and twist the wire to secure.

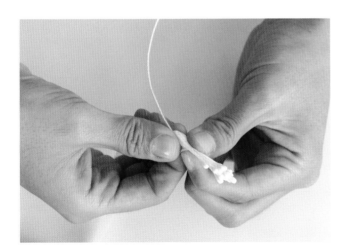

3 Wrap the bottom half of the stamen bunch with floral tape and continue wrapping down the length of the cloth-covered floral wire about 3"–5" (7.5cm–12.5cm).

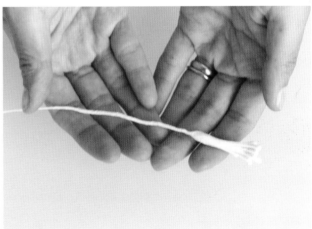

4 Trim the excess wires if necessary.

Finishing the Back With Felt

Whether the piece is wired onto a comb or headband or hand-sewn, a felt backing is a nice way to finish the project. It also prevents wires from snagging your hair and can help reinforce the piece.

YOU WILL NEED

1½"–2" (4cm–5cm) wide strip of felt or interfacing approximately 1"–2" (2.5cm–5cm) longer than what you want to cover

scissors

fabric glue

Cut the felt to extend from ½"–1" (1cm–2.5cm) on every side of the comb or portion of the piece you want to cover. A rounded oval or rectangular shape works well. Glue the felt onto the section you want to cover using fabric glue. If you are covering a comb, cut a slit in the middle of the felt and slide the felt onto the teeth of the comb. Glue the felt down.

Opening and Closing a Jump Ring

Jump rings are great for joining beads and clasps. They are very simple to use, and opening and closing them is an easy technique to perfect.

YOU WILL NEED

2 pairs of chain-nose pliers

1 jump ring

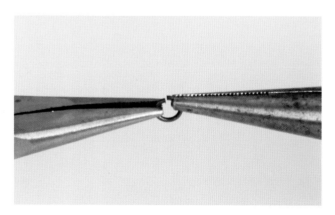

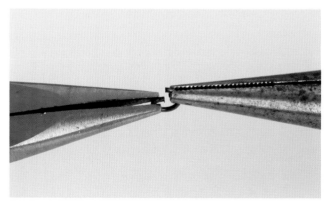

1 Grip the jump ring on either side of the opening with two pairs of chain-nose pliers.

2 Open the jump ring by moving one end toward you and the other end away from you. Don't pull or push on the jump ring.

To close, move the ends in the exact opposite direction until they meet. Again, do not pull or push on the jump ring to close it.

Wire Wrapping Beads

Using beads and crystals to accent pieces is lovely and easy. One way to include beads in your projects is by wrapping them with wire.

YOU WILL NEED

craft or shaping wire (28-gauge works well for the projects in this book)

beads

wire cutters

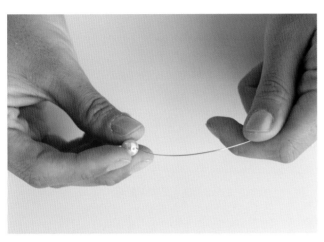

1 String a bead onto the wire.

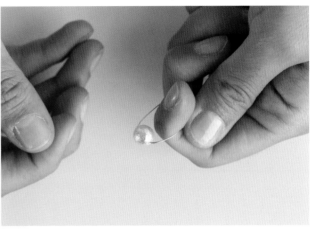

2 Place your left index finger between the wires and have the bead positioned on top of your finger.

3 Use your right hand to grasp the bead and begin twisting.

4 Continue twisting the wire until the desired length of twisted wire is achieved.

Wrapping Wire and Creating Loops

This technique is useful when joining beads to chain. It is simple, but practice is definitely helpful. Try cutting a few lengths of wire and practicing a few times to get it right.

YOU WILL NEED

beads

28-gauge shaping wire

wire cutters

half-round pliers

1 Slide a small bead onto the center of a piece of wire. Thread both ends of the wire through another bead and pull through.

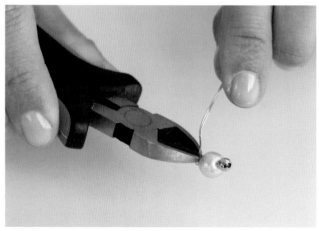

2 Using the half-round pliers, grip the wire close to the bead. Press the pliers together to create a 90-degree bend in the wire.

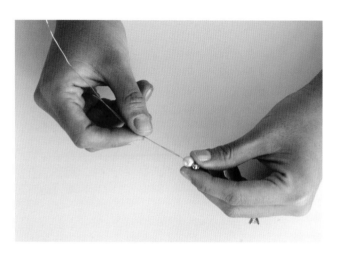

3 Wrap the ends of the wire around the right angle bend two to three times.

4 Trim off the excess wire and tuck the cut end into the wire.

Cutting Petals Freehand

Becoming proficient at cutting petals freehand will greatly increase the speed at which you can cut flowers. To create even petals, make evenly distributed straight cuts in the circles and then round the corners. You will need to make the same number of cuts as petals needed. For example, a flower with five petals will require five straight cuts.

1 Make a straight cut in the circle, starting at the edge and ending about a third of the way from the center of the circle.

2 Visualize the circle as a clock and treat the first cut as twelve o'clock. Make an identical cut at five o'clock. Then make a cut directly between the first and second cut (about three o'clock). Make a fourth cut at seven o'clock and then another cut between seven and twelve o'clock.

3 Round the corners of each cut section to form petals.

CHAPTER TWO

Flowers

I LOVE THE LOOK and feel of flowers. With a look that is both modern and vintage at the same time, they can turn any piece into a truly amazing creation. They are wonderful to give and receive, and they are absolutely stunning to wear.

I started pressing my own handmade flowers several years ago when I found myself limited by premade fabric flowers. I wanted to have greater control over the materials, colors and sizes of the flowers. By creating flowers from scratch, you can make pieces that are exactly as you envision them. You can choose the colors to match a favorite cardigan or special dress. In this chapter, you will learn how to use basic flower-pressing skills to create dimensional and realistic flowers, as well as how to create flowers by hand-curling and hand-sewing.

GOLDEN FLORAL
WRIST CORSAGE

This dainty floral piece is both simple and eye-catching. The bloom is created using old millinery and basic sewing techniques. The design is one of my favorite flower styles to create and can also be worn as a headband or belt if you use longer lengths of ribbon. You can use different colors of fabric and experiment with different fabric weights to create a variety of flowers.

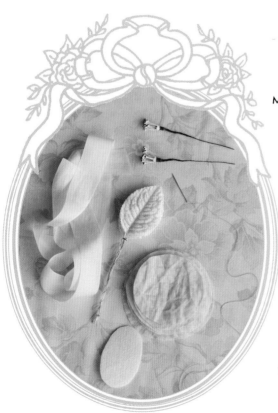

MATERIALS

12" × 20" (30cm × 51cm) of cotton linen, starched

15" (38cm) of 1"–1½" (2.5cm–4cm) wide ribbon

2 stamen clusters

2 velvet millinery leaves

1½" × 3" (4cm × 8cm) rectangular piece of felt or nonfusible interfacing

TOOLS

needle

thread

scissors

pointed embroidery scissors or wooden awl

millinery irons or dapping set

foam pad covered with cotton

1 Cut the cotton fabric into six 5" (12.5cm) squares. This makes proportioning the fabric easier.

2 Use scissors to cut the corners of the squares to round them and create circles.

3 Make six circles, with the smallest being approximately 3" (8cm) in diameter, gradually increasing in size, with the largest being approximately 4½" (11cm) in diameter.

4 Cut five rounded petals into each circle. You can either freehand cut them or sketch a five-petal flower onto each circle to guide your cutting (see *Cutting Petals Freehand* on page 27).

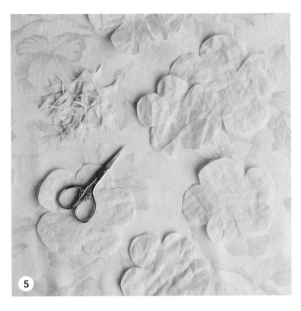

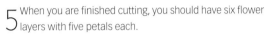

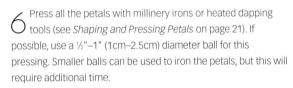

5 When you are finished cutting, you should have six flower layers with five petals each.

6 Press all the petals with millinery irons or heated dapping tools (see *Shaping and Pressing Petals* on page 21). If possible, use a ½"–1" (1cm–2.5cm) diameter ball for this pressing. Smaller balls can be used to iron the petals, but this will require additional time.

7 When stacked, the smallest petal layer should be on the top and the largest on the bottom, similar to nesting dolls.

8 Using a sharp pair of scissors or a wooden awl, carefully poke a hole in the center of each of the six layers of petals.

9 Pull the two stamen clusters through the hole in the smallest petal layer.

10 Continue pulling the stamens through the petal layers from smallest to largest until the stamens have gone through all six layers. Make sure each additional petal layer is staggered in between the previous petal layer to create a fuller looking flower. Set aside.

11 Twist the wires of the velvet millinery leaves together, joining them at their bases.

12 Hand-stitch the velvet leaves onto one end of the felt, leaving about 1" (2.5cm) of felt beneath the leaves to help support them.

13 Using sharp scissors or a wooden awl, poke two holes about ½" (1cm) apart into the end of the felt opposite the leaves. You will use these holes to attach the flower.

14 Insert the ends of the stamens from the flower into one of the holes in the felt from top to bottom. Pull the stamens through the second hole so the ends are on the top side.

15 To finish the piece, wrap the wire ends of the stamen around themselves at the base of the flower to secure. Hand-sew the bottom petal layer to the felt to conceal the wire.

16 To finish the piece, hand-sew the center of the ribbon to the underside of the piece.

BLUSHING SILK
PETALS HAIR COMB

This lovely and feminine hair comb is lightweight and easy to wear. I especially like the overall texture and depth. It requires basic petal-pressing techniques and repetition, but it is a relatively easy piece to create and is sure to impress.

MATERIALS

8" × 20" (20cm × 51cm) of silk chiffon

8" × 20" (20cm × 51cm) of silk habotai, starched

2" × 5" (5cm × 13cm) of felt or nonfusible interfacing, cut into a crescent shape

1 wire comb, approximately 2½" (6cm) long

TOOLS

needle

thread

scissors

millinery irons or dapping set

foam pad covered with cotton fabric

1 Cut the silk habotai and silk chiffon into squares approximately 3½"–4" (9cm–10cm) across until you have twenty squares of each fabric.

2 Separate the fabrics so you have ten stacks of silk habotai with two squares each. Do the same for the silk chiffon. By making stacks, you will save time by cutting through multiple layers at once.

3 Fold one stack in half.

4 Fold the stack in half again.

5 Fold the stack on the diagonal.

6 You should now have a triangle-shaped piece of folded silk.

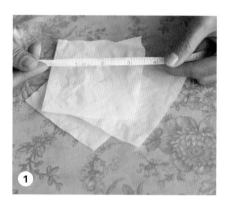

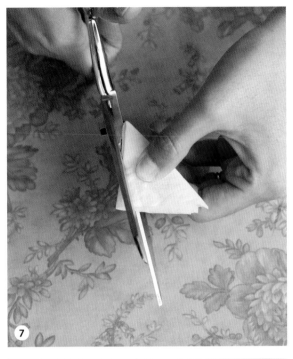

7 Cut a rounded petal through all layers, making sure to cut the open edges and not the folded corner. To make this easier, grip the folded fabric at the bottom corner where there are folds.

8 When you unfold the diagonal fold, the fabric should look like a heart.

9 When fully open, the fabric will have eight petal points. Repeat Steps 3–8 until all silk habotai and silk chiffon stacks are cut into petals. Set the silk chiffon petals aside.

10 Press all ten stacks of silk habotai petals with a ½" (1cm) millinery iron or dapping tool.

11 Begin hand-sewing the pressed petals onto the crescent-shaped felt, starting at one end.

12 Continue sewing silk habotai petals onto the felt, mixing in silk chiffon petals until you have sewn all petals.

13 On the back, hand-sew a comb to the felt to complete the piece.

PATTERNED SILK FLOWERED HEADBAND

This dramatic style can be made with a variety of materials and prints. Since the petals are wired, you can shape them to create a custom fit or form. If possible, use a crinkle silk chiffon fabric, as it adds texture to the petals without needing to press them with millinery irons.

MATERIALS

10" × 13" (25cm × 33cm) of patterned silk, starched

2 stamen clusters

1 fabric-covered headband

an assortment of small velvet or silk flowers and leaves

5 pieces of cloth stem wires, cut 6" (15cm) long

fabric glue

3"–4" (7.5cm–10cm) long strip of felt, cut to the width of the headband

floral tape

TOOLS

scissors

wire cutters

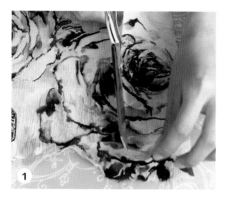

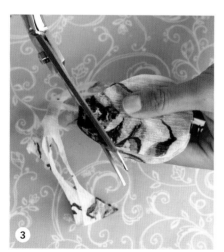

1 Cut the patterned silk fabric into three 3" × 12" (7.5cm × 30.5cm) strips.

2 When all fabric is cut into strips, fold each strip in half widthwise, then in half again widthwise, resulting in a folded square of fabric.

3 Using scissors, freehand cut teardrop-shaped petals from a folded square of fabric. Folding the fabric helps reduce the amount of cuts required to create the petals. You should have a few extra petals, which you can save for another project.

4 Stack the petals into five piles of two petals each.

5 Carefully apply a strip of fabric glue to one of the cloth stem wires, leaving about 3" (7.5cm) free of glue.

6 Separate one pair of silk petals. Press the glued cloth stem wire into the center of a single petal, making sure the wire does not extend past the edge of the petal.

7 Press the second petal directly over the top of the first petal and cloth stem wire, aligning the petals and concealing the wire.

8 Repeat Steps 5–7 until you have five wired teardrop-shaped petals. Set aside to dry.

9 After the glue has dried, gently grip the base of a wired petal with one hand and bend a curve into the petal with the other hand. Try to avoid sharp bends.

10 Repeat Step 9 until all five petals are shaped.

11 Bunch two stamen clusters and one of the wired petals together. Wrap floral tape around the stems a few times to secure.

12 Add each of the remaining petals to the bunch, securing each with floral tape. Overlap each petal by about ¼" (6mm) over the previous petal to create a full flower without gaps.

13 Using the wire cutters, cut four of the cloth stem wires close to the floral tape, leaving the ends of the stamen wires and one cloth stem wire. Cutting the wires reduces bulk and makes attaching the flower to a headband easier.

14 Choose a small assortment of accent flowers. If you use flowers with wires, wrap the wires together to create a bunch. If your flowers do not have wires, you can bunch them and secure them with floral tape.

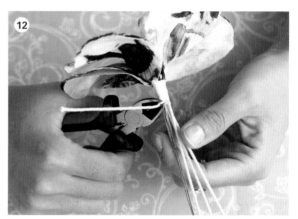

15

16

17

15 Add one or two leaves to the bunch of small flowers by wrapping the wire or using floral tape.

16 Make a leaf bunch and another flower bunch.

17 Begin wrapping the wire ends of the bunch of flowers from Step 15 around the headband to secure. Start about 2" (5cm) from the end of the band. If your bunches do not have wires, you can hand sew them onto the headband.

18 Attach the silk-patterned flower to the headband, facing it outward on the side you prefer to wear the adornment on your head.

Repeat Step 17 on the other side of the flower, using the leaf bunch from Step 16. Finish by gluing a strip of felt to the underside of the band, which will secure the wires and create a clean finish (see *Finishing the Back With Felt* on page 24).

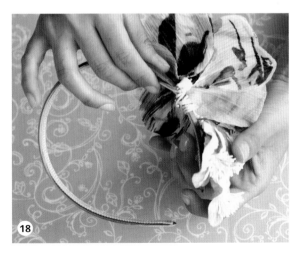

18

PETITE SILK CLUSTER FLOWER COMB

This comb is the perfect little piece to wear every day or on special occasions. You can select several small premade silk flowers of your choice. Try to find small flowers that are 1" to 2" (2.5cm to 5cm) wide. This project requires petal-pressing and basic wire-wrapping skills.

MATERIALS

6–8 stamen clusters

3–4 small, premade silk flowers

(4) 2½" (6cm) squares of brown silk or cotton fabric, starched

(4) 2½" (6cm) squares of pink silk or cotton fabric, starched

2 velvet leaves or artificial silk leaves

1" × 2" (2.5cm × 5cm) piece of soft felt or interfacing

1 comb, approximately 1½"–2" (2cm–4cm) long

TOOLS

glue

scissors

millinery irons or dapping set

foam pad covered with cotton fabric

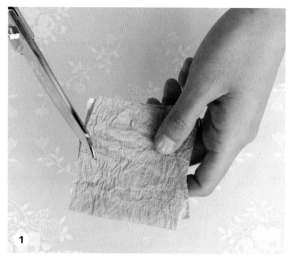

1. Stack two to three squares of silk fabric and cut five rounded petal segments into the squares. Cutting through more than one layer at a time saves time, but you can cut through just one layer at a time if you prefer.

2. Repeat Step 1 with all squares of fabric in both colors until you have eight separate petal layers.

3. Using the millinery iron or dapping tools, press all the petals (see *Shaping and Pressing Petals* on page 21). If the fabric is not too thick, you can press through two to four layers simultaneously to save time.

4. Stack two petal layers of the same color and, using a sharp pair of scissors or wooden awl, poke a small hole in the centers. Repeat with the remaining pressed petals.

5. Insert one to two stamen clusters through two petal layers of the same color.

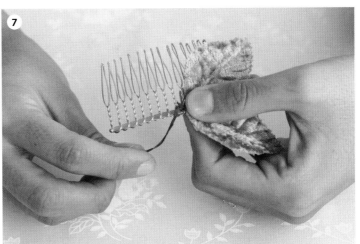

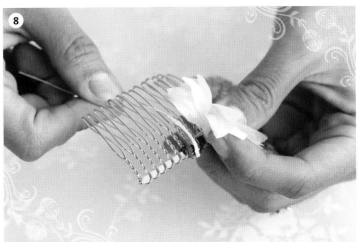

6 Repeat Step 5 with the remaining petal layers.

7 Wrap the wire ends of the velvet or silk leaves around the comb. If your leaves do not have wire, you can hand-stitch them to the comb.

8 Select a premade silk flower and attach it to the comb. Some smaller flowers come with wire already attached. If yours does not, you can hand sew or glue it to the comb.

9 Repeat Step 8, mixing premade flowers with the handmade flowers until all flowers are used or the comb is covered.

Using glue, attach a small piece of felt to the back side of the comb to finish (see *Finishing the Back With Felt* on page 24).

BLOSSOM AND PEARL COMB

With its tiny blossoms and delicate branches, this petite comb will add the prettiest accent in your hair. This piece has a very dainty feel and can be made with real or faux pearls. You can also add more blossoms if you'd like a larger piece. This project utilizes wire-wrapping and petal-pressing. The individual wire-wrapped beads can be bent slightly to create a very whimsical finished arrangement, similar to real cherry blossoms.

MATERIALS

(5) 2" (5cm) squares of silk or cotton fabric, starched

1 small comb

26" (66cm) 28-gauge craft wire

5–8 freshwater pearls or beads

5 small round beads, approximately 3mm–5mm

TOOLS

wire cutters

scissors

millinery iron or dapping set

foam pad covered with cotton fabric

fabric glue

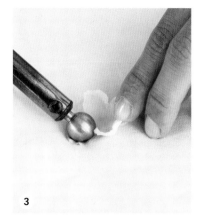

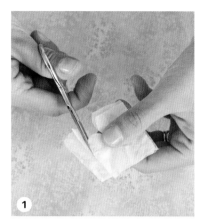

1 Stack two to three squares of silk or cotton fabric and cut five-petal flowers. You can also cut through a single square at a time if you prefer.

2 Continue cutting until you have five flowers.

3 Press the flower petals. You can press two to three layers simultaneously to save time.

4 Poke a small hole through the center of each flower using a sharp pair of pointed scissors or wooden awl.

5 Align one end of the 28-gauge wire about halfway along the top bar of the comb.

6 Holding the wire against the bar of the comb, begin wrapping the wire around itself and the bar of the comb. Make sure to overlap the wire to secure it. Wrap it around the comb three to five times.

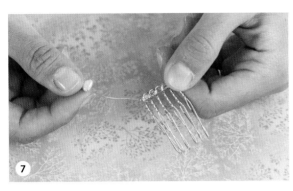

7 Slide one pearl onto the wire, stopping about 1"–1½" (2.5cm–4cm) before the comb.

8 Holding the pearl in one hand, cross the wire over itself and begin twisting.

9 Twist the wire until it is tightly wound. Wrap the wire around the bar of the comb once or twice to secure it.

10 Insert the wire through a pressed flower from back to front.

11 Slide one small bead onto the wire.

12 Bring the wire end back through the hole in the flower, this time from front to back.

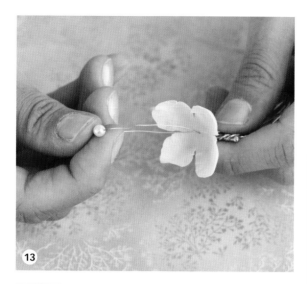

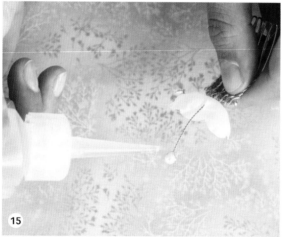

13 Adjust the wire until the pearl is about 1"–2" (2.5cm–5cm) from the bar of the comb. You can vary this length as desired for a longer or shorter branch.

14 Holding the comb in one hand, use the other hand to hold the bead and twist until the wire it tightly twisted. Wrap the end of the wire around the bar of the comb once or twice to secure it.

15 Add a very small dot of glue to the base of the wired bead.

16 Slide the flower up the twisted wire to the base of the glued bead to secure the petal to the bead.

17 Bend the wire with your fingers to create a curved branch.

18 Repeat Steps 7–17 until all flowers and pearls are added to the comb. Wrap the end of the wire around the comb a few times.

19 Using wire cutters, trim the wire, leaving ¼" (6mm) excess.

20 Using your finger or pliers, tuck the wire end into the wrapped wire on the comb to finish the piece.

BLOSSOM AND PEARL NECKLACE

This delicate piece is similar to the *Blossom and Pearl Comb* (see page 52) but is adapted to be worn as a necklace and has crystal beads for an extra bit of sparkle. You can add more or fewer blossoms, pearls or crystals as desired. This project utilizes a store-bought bead wire with magnetic clasps already attached, making it a breeze to add the wired blossoms and beads. Once secured onto the bead wire, it's ready to wear and is easy to take on and off.

MATERIALS

(8) 1½" (4cm) squares of silk or cotton fabric, starched

(1) 18" (45.5cm) piece of bead wire with attached magnetic clasps

45" (114cm) of 28-gauge craft wire, cut into five 9" (23cm) pieces

5–8 freshwater pearls or beads

(10) 4mm Swarovski crystal or clear faceted beads

17 small round beads, approximately 3mm–5mm

TOOLS

wire cutters

scissors

millinery iron or dapping set

foam pad covered with cotton fabric

fabric glue

1 Stack two to three squares of silk or cotton fabric and cut five-petal flowers. You can also cut through a single square at a time if you prefer. Make eight flowers.

2 Press the flower petals. You can press two to three layers simultaneously to save time. Use a small millinery iron for these small flowers.

3 Using a sharp pair of scissors or wooden awl, poke a hole in the center of the flower.

4 Slide a crystal onto the center of a piece of wire. Bend the wire in half and hold the crystal in one hand.

5 Twist the wire tightly until the twisted portion is about ½"–1" (1cm–2.5cm) long.

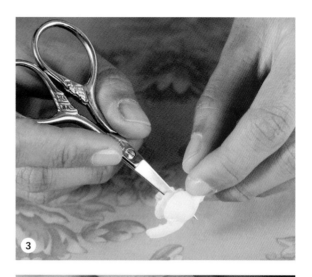

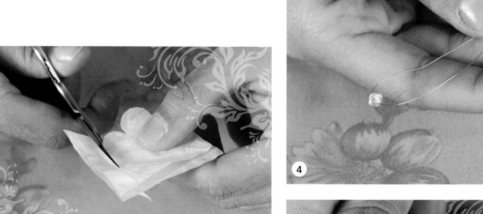

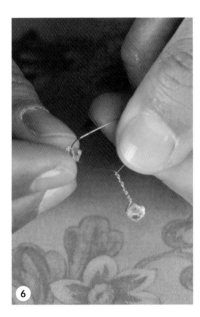

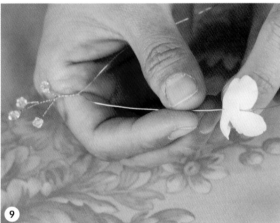

6 Slide a second crystal onto one of the twisted wire ends. As you did in Step 4, slide on a second crystal, stopping about ½"–1" (1cm–2.5cm) from the twisted portion. Bend the wire down around each side of the crystal and twist the wire.

7 Your crystals should look like a letter Y.

8 Add additional crystals in this manner until you have four to six crystals on the wire. Alternate the end you add the crystal to, creating a fern-like pattern. After twisting on a crystal, twist both wires together for about ½" (1cm). This will create a branch-like effect. Finish the branch of crystals by twisting the wires together for about ½" (1cm).

9 Slide one end of the wire through a pressed flower from back to front.

10 Slide one small bead onto the wire.

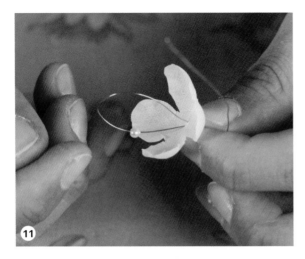

11 Bend the wire back toward the flower and insert the wire through the hole from front to back.

12 Pull the wire through until the flower and bead are about ½"–1" (1cm–2.5cm) from the last twisted section of wire. Holding the bead in one hand and bracing the wire, twist the bead until the wire is tightly wound.

13 Using fabric glue, add a small drop of glue to the base of the wired bead.

14 Slide the fabric petal toward the bead to adhere it to the glue and secure.

15 Twist the two wires together for about ½"–1" (1cm–2.5cm).

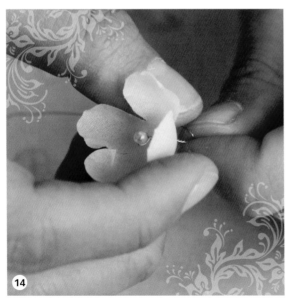

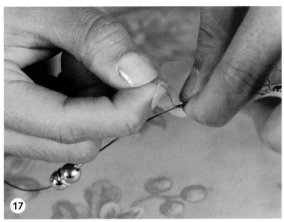

16 Repeat Steps 4–15 with three more pieces of wire. You can mix freshwater pearls, crystals, beads and flowers. Each wired segment can be different. When finished, you will have four branches. Join the branches by twisting the ends of one segment to the beginning of another until they form one piece.

17 Using the ends of the last wire segment, twist the floral and bead segment onto the bead wire necklace. Tuck in the wire ends.

18 Begin at one end of the floral and bead segment and wrap the last wire piece around it and the bead wire.

19 Continue to lash the floral and bead segment to the bead wire until the entire piece is secured. You may decide to leave 2"–3" (5cm–7.5cm) of the design free so it bends away like a real floral branch. Trim and tuck in the wire ends as needed to finish.

OVERSIZED HANDMADE SILK FLOWER COMB

A stunning and statement-making flower is the focal point of this amazing headpiece. The flower is completely handmade and over-the-top in a very good way. The piece would be perfect for a party, wedding or engagement shoot. This flower is realistic-looking and doesn't require any special tools or techniques. Try to find a fabric with a range of colors to create a natural-looking flower with depth and dimension. Use a slightly darker fabric for the center of the flower and lighter fabric for the outer petals.

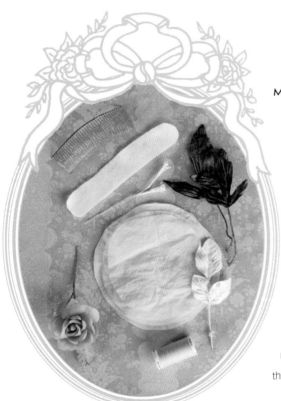

MATERIALS

2 different velvet leaf sprigs

2 stamen clusters

5 silk or cotton fabric circles, starched: 6" (15cm), 5½" (14cm), 5" (12.5cm), 4½" (11.5cm), 4" (10cm) and 3" (7.5cm) diameters respectively

1 small premade silk flower

5"–8" (13cm–20cm) long comb

2" × 8" (5cm × 20cm) piece of felt, or piece large enough to cover the length of the comb

TOOLS

fabric glue

scissors

needle

thread

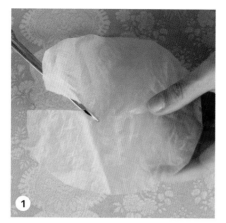

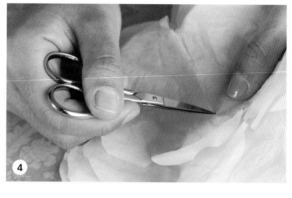

1 Cut five rounded petal segments in each circle of fabric.

2 Using your index finger and thumb, pinch the edge of one petal. Roll and curl the petal edge with your finger and thumb. It is easier to move your index finger toward you. You may need to do this a few times per petal to achieve the desired result. Alternatively, you can curl the petal edge using a pair of scissors or the edge of a table.

3 Continue curling all the petals until all five layers have curled petal edges.

4 Using a sharp pair of scissors or wooden awl, poke a hole in the centers of all the petal layers. You can do this through multiple layers at once or one at a time.

5 Insert two stamen clusters through the two smallest petal layers. Pull the ends through until only the stamens are visible on the top side.

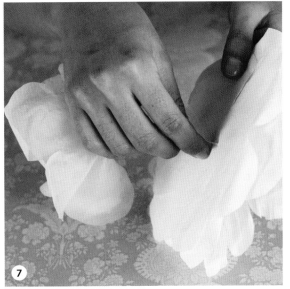

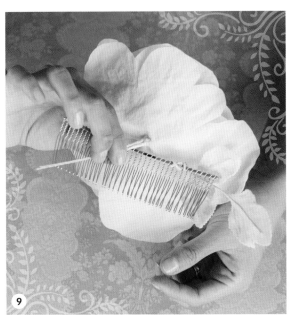

6 From the underside, pinch the petals around the stamens and stitch them together. This will create fullness in the final flower by keeping the petals lifted, as opposed to lying flat.

7 Slide the next three petal layers onto the stamen wires, staggering them from small to large.

8 Wrap the wire ends of the velvet leaves to the end of the comb. If your leaves do not have wires, you can hand sew them to the comb.

9 Wire or sew the largest flower to the center of the comb. Repeat for the premade flower, placing it slightly off center next to the largest flower. Add leaves to either side of the flowers. Finish by attaching a piece of felt to the back with fabric glue for a clean finish (see *Finishing the Back With Felt* on page 24).

CHAPTER THREE

Feathers

SOFT AND LOVELY, feathers are a unique addition to your accessories assortment. Some feathers are wispy and blow delicately in the breeze, while others are more structured and can be formed into beautiful, modern shapes. I love to create feathery pieces for brides and individuals attending special events, such as New Year's Eve parties or The Royal Ascot. Larger feathery pieces make a statement and are perfect for photo shoots, but using small feathers can make for surprisingly wearable everyday jewelry. Feathers have a whimsical and ethereal aesthetic that appeals to a wide array of personal styles.

FEATHER SPRAY BROOCH

This design is simple, yet playful, and can be worn on clothing or attached to a favorite purse or pair of shoes. It is soft and moves as you do. You can use a variety of feather colors and types. Wispy ostrich feathers work very well, but you can also experiment with stiffer, structured feathers for a more sophisticated look.

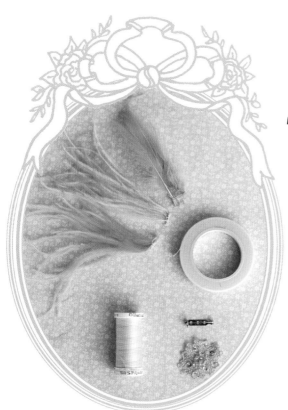

MATERIALS

1 piece of small lace, approximately 1" (2.5cm) wide

2–3 strips of various feathers, strung, approximately ½" (1cm) strung length

1 brooch pin

TOOLS

scissors

needle

thread

1 Align the ends of the feathers together. You may need to trim some of the feathers.

2 Wrap the bases of the feathers together with floral tape.

3 Wrap the lace around the base of the feathers.

4 Hand-stitch the lace onto the feathers by piercing the needle through the floral tape and lace a few times.

5 Choose one side to be the front side of the brooch. Hand-stitch a brooch pin to the back side to finish.

FEATHER AND BURNT SILK PETAL HAIR CLIP

Adorn your locks with a very romantic hair clip made with feathers and some carefully singed silk petals. This piece would be perfect for everyday wear. It is small and lightweight and will definitely make you feel prettier the moment you put it on. It can be made with a variety of feathers, but it helps to use flatter and wider feathers.

MATERIALS

5" (12.5cm) square of silk or cotton fabric, starched

10–14 flat, broad feathers (goose feathers are recommended)

1 lace appliqué, about 1"–2" (2.5cm–5cm) across

1 alligator clip

5–10 assorted small beads

2 pieces of teardrop-shaped felt, approximately 2" × 3" (5cm × 7.5cm)

TOOLS

scissors

needle

thread

lighter, candle or stove top burner

1 Make five equally spaced folds lengthwise in the silk or cotton fabric so each fold is 1" apart.

2 Fold the fabric in half widthwise.

3 Carefully cut a long petal shape, similar to an elongated oval, from the folded fabric. Make sure to cut through all the layers. It should be about 1"–1¼" (2.5cm–3cm) long and ½"–¾" (1cm–2cm) wide.

4 Cut a tapered end on one end of the petals

5 There are a couple of ways you can burn the edges of the petals. You can slowly burn the edges with a lighter or candle, keeping the petals at a distance above the flame. You can also hold the petals with tongs above a stovetop. The stovetop method creates a softer burned edge, and the candle method creates a more charred edge. With either method, be very careful not to burn yourself or keep the fabric over the heat source for too long. You don't want it to catch on fire. Rather, you want the edges to singe slightly. Singe all the petals.

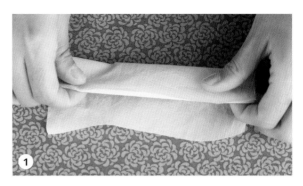

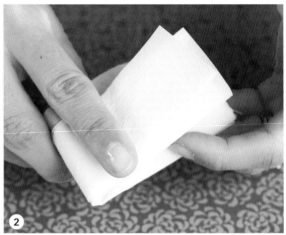

6 Trim the feathers, aiming for lengths between 1½" and 3" (4cm and 7.5cm) long.

7 Begin gluing the feathers onto the wider end of a teardrop-shaped felt piece.

8 Glue a second feather next to the first, slightly overlapping it over the first feather. Repeat until you reach the opposite side of the felt piece.

9 Glue on a second row of feathers, overlapping the second row over the first row and overlapping each feather in the row as you did in the first row. Repeat this process until the felt piece is covered (approximately three rows). Inspect the finished feather pad to make sure there are no blank spots.

10 Place the lace appliqué toward the tapered end of the feather pad and hand-stitch it on.

11 Sew the first singed petal about a third of the way up the feather pad, starting from the tapered end. You will be layering the petals in a similar manner to the feathers; however, you don't need to place them exactly. A more artistic placement looks better.

12 Continue layering and sewing on petals.

13 When all the petals are sewn on to cover the lower third of the feather pad, hand-sew the beads and crystals to the piece. Try to cluster them more densely at the tip of the piece, and thin and scatter them as you move away from the tip.

14 Fold the second piece of teardrop-shaped felt in half lengthwise.

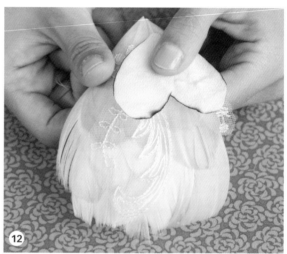

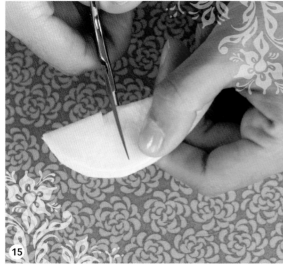

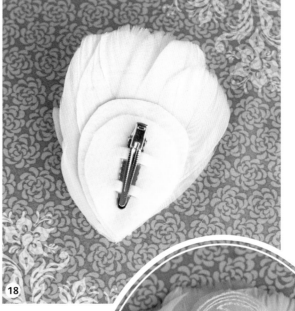

15 Make four cuts in the folded felt. Think of them as two pairs of cuts. Each cut in a pair should be about ¼" (6mm) apart and about ¼" (6mm) long (½" [1cm] when unfolded). The pairs should be about ½"–¾" (1cm–3cm) apart.

16 Inspect the cuts to ensure the alligator clip will fit through them.

17 Slide the top portion of the alligator clip through the first pair of slits and then through the second pair of slits.

18 Glue the felt with the alligator clip onto the felt side of the feather pad to finish the piece.

SOFT FEATHER DANGLE EARRINGS

Soft and delicate, these wispy earrings are so lightweight you'll forget you're wearing them. They move and dance with the slightest breeze and will tickle our neck as you walk. Find any feather that is not too large and has a good main stem. Goose feathers are used in this project, but rooster feathers or guinea fowl feathers would also be lovely.

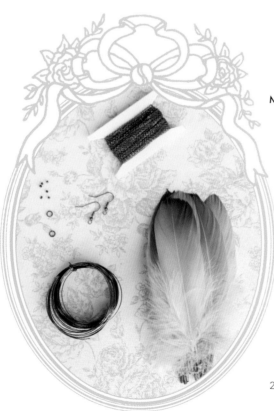

MATERIALS

6 small brass crimp beads

12" (30.5cm) of brass chain, cut into 6 pieces, 2 of each size: 2½" (6cm), 2" (5cm) and 1½" (4cm)

6" (15cm) of brass colored wire, cut into (2) 3" (7.5cm) pieces

2 hook ear wires

(2) 5mm jump rings

(6) 3mm jump rings

TOOLS

half-round pliers

wire cutters

scissors

round-nose pliers

2 pairs of chain-nose pliers

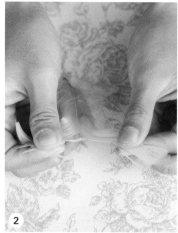

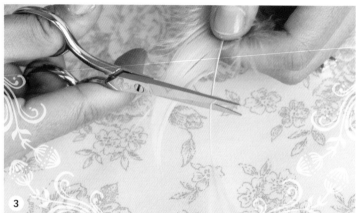

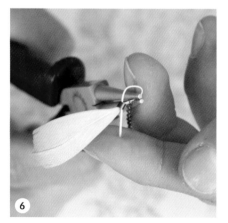

1 Hold the feather in your left hand, about ½"–1" (1cm–2.5cm) from the tip, and separate the filaments using your right hand.

2 Firmly pull away the extra feather parts that you won't need. You can remove all the filaments on either side of teh feather's spine until there is about ½" (13mm) remaining. To do this, hold the feather filaments between your thumb and index finger and, with the tip of the feather away facing from you, pull the feather filaments toward your body. Repeat with the other half of the feather.

3 Cut the end of the feather so there is about 1" (2.5cm) of stripped feather spine remaining. Repeat Steps 1–3 for five more feathers for a total of six stripped feathers.

4 Slide a crimp bead down the stripped feather until it is nearly touching the soft filaments.

5 Attach a 3mm jump ring to the last link of any of the segments of chain. Insert the feather with the crimp bead through the jump ring.

6 Grip the feather with the round-nose pliers very close to the chain. Loop the end of the feather over the top of the pliers and through the crimp bead. Pull through until there is just a small loop.

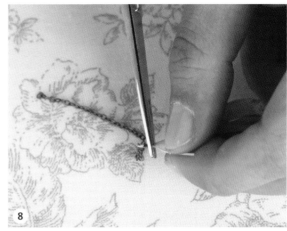

7 Firmly press and flatten the crimp bead with the chain-nose pliers to secure the feather.

8 Use a pair of scissors to trim off the extra length of feather spine as close to the crimp bead as possible.

9 Repeat Steps 4–8 for all the stripped feathers.

10 Separate the feathers into two groups with three different lengths of chain in each. Each group will form one earring. Thread a 3" (7.5cm) piece of wire through the last link of each chain in one group of feathers.

11 Allow the feathers to hang in the center of the wire. Using the round-nose pliers, grip the wire just to the right of the chains.

12

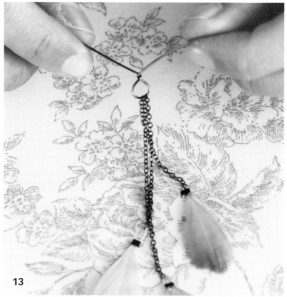

13

14

12 Loop one end of the wire around the top of the pliers to create a loop.

13 Twist the wires two to three times at the base of the loop.

14 Use the half-round pliers to create a second loop by wrapping one end of wire around the top of the pliers.

15 After the wire is wrapped around the top of the pliers, twist the end a couple times between both loops.

15

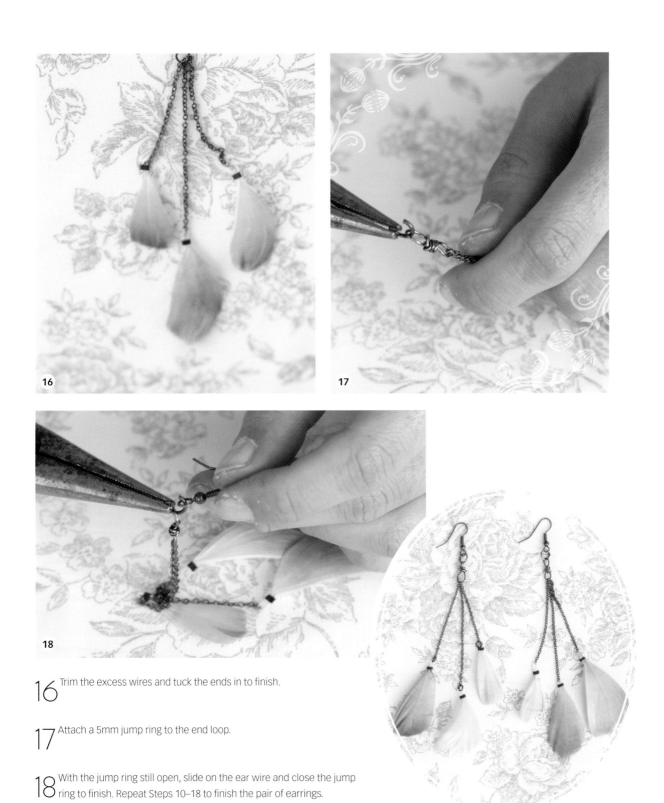

16 Trim the excess wires and tuck the ends in to finish.

17 Attach a 5mm jump ring to the end loop.

18 With the jump ring still open, slide on the ear wire and close the jump ring to finish. Repeat Steps 10–18 to finish the pair of earrings.

PINK CURVED FEATHER NECKLACE

Softly sweeping across your neck, this lovely feather necklace is very modern and unique. You can make the feather portion longer or shorter if you like, and you can use any color of feathers you find. You'll use layering and feather-curling techniques in this project, and it is relatively quick and easy to finish. The project as pictured uses both flat goose feathers and a larger peacock wing feather (the brown speckled feather), but you can use any larger feather you'd like.

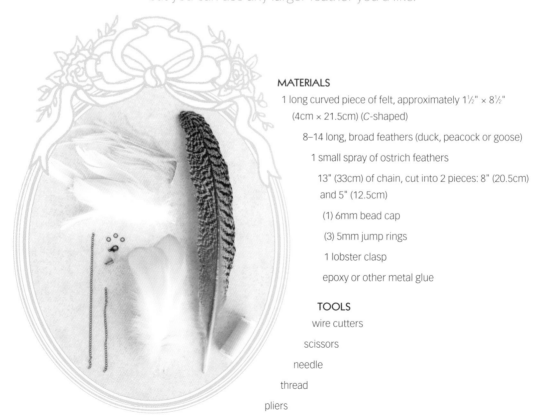

MATERIALS

1 long curved piece of felt, approximately 1½" × 8½" (4cm × 21.5cm) (*C*-shaped)

8–14 long, broad feathers (duck, peacock or goose)

1 small spray of ostrich feathers

13" (33cm) of chain, cut into 2 pieces: 8" (20.5cm) and 5" (12.5cm)

(1) 6mm bead cap

(3) 5mm jump rings

1 lobster clasp

epoxy or other metal glue

TOOLS

wire cutters

scissors

needle

thread

pliers

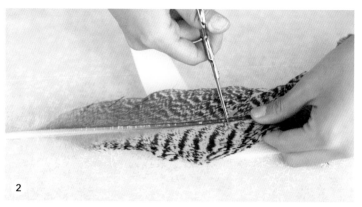

1 If you're using a large feather, curl the feather to create a pleasing overall shape. If the main spine is very thick, you can curl it by slightly cracking it between your fingers. Pinch it, starting from the tip and spacing your pinches every ½" (1cm). Use your thumbnail to press until you hear or feel it crack. You don't want it to break, so be careful. Continue curling and pinching down the length of the feather.

2 If your feather is longer than 5" (12.5cm), trim it to about 5" (12.5cm) to make assembling easier.

3 Apply a line of glue on the back of the feather along its spine.

4 Press the feather firmly onto the end of the felt and hold until it has adhered.

5 If you have medium-sized feathers about 4"–8" (10cm–20.5cm) long, trim them so they are about 3"–4" (7.5cm–10cm) long.

6 Place a small but adequate amount of glue on the back side of a medium-sized feather, both near and on the tip.

7 Place the feather on the piece, layering it on top of the first feather so about 1"–2" (2.5cm–5cm) of the first feather is still protruding.

8 Add additional medium-sized feathers in the same manner until you have added three to four feathers.

9 Split the strip of ostrich feathers into two groups and glue the ends of one bunch together. Adhere the bunch onto the piece so the unglued ends overlap the previous feathers.

10 Repeat Steps 6–9 until you have almost covered the felt with feathers. Leave about ¼" (6mm) of the end of the felt exposed. Set aside.

6

7

8

9

10

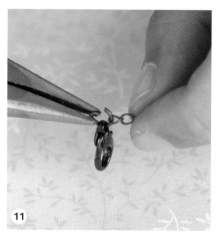

11

12

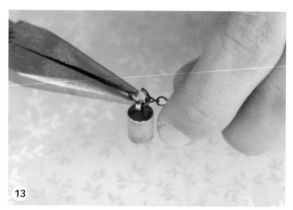

13

11 Open a jump ring and slide on the last link of the 8" (20.5cm) length of chain and the lobster clasp. Close the jump ring and set aside.

12 Open the second jump ring and attach the bead cap.

13 Attach the last link of the 5" (12.5cm) length of chain to the open jump ring. Close the jump ring.

14 Attach another jump ring to the opposite end of the 5" (12.5cm) length of chain. Set aside.

15 Trim the exposed end of the felt if needed to ensure it will fit into the bead cap. Next, apply a small amount of epoxy or other suitable metal glue to the exposed end of the felt.

14

15

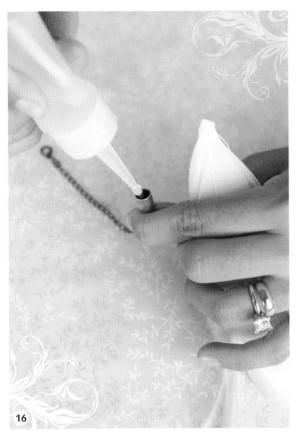

16 Squeeze a small amount of epoxy or metal glue into the bead cap.

17 Insert the glued end of the felt into the bead cap. Clean away any excess glue before it dries. Let it dry.

18 Using a needle and thread, hand-stitch the remaining chain with the lobster clasp onto the opposite end of felt. Stich it to the underside of the felt using the jump ring you attached. Tie off the thread tightly to finish the piece.

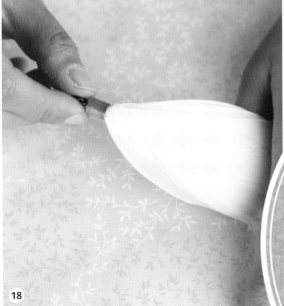

LACE EMBELLISHED BOBBY PIN

This sweet and small bobby pin can be made in a variety of colors depending on the lace you choose. It is as pretty as it is functional: It keeps the hair off your face while adding a bit of ladylike interest to your hairstyle. You can customize it by using different beads, buttons or feathers. Alternatively, you can sew the piece onto a brooch pin instead of a bobby pin. This project is simple in its construction and a breeze to create and wear.

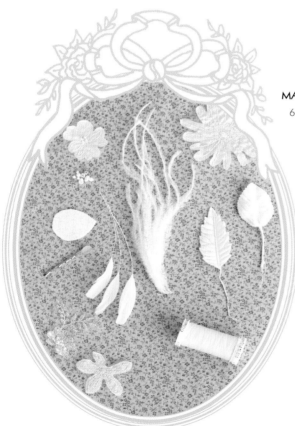

MATERIALS

6–8 ostrich feather pieces with longer filaments

3 stripped rooster feathers or other small feathers

1 bobby pin

2 velvet leaves

3–4 small floral lace appliqués

6–9 small beads, crystals or rhinestones

small piece of teardrop-shaped felt, approximately 1½" (4cm) long

TOOLS

glue

scissors

needle

thread

1 Twist the wires of the velvet leaves together to join them. If your leaves do not have wires, you can hand sew them together.

2 Layer the lace appliqués together with the largest piece on the bottom and the smallest on top.

3 Hand-stitch the lace together.

4 Hand-stitch an assortment of crystals and beads to the center of the lace layers.

5 Carefully create a hole in the felt using a pair of sharp scissors or a wooden awl.

6 Insert one bar of the bobby pin through the hole in the felt. The open end of the bobby pin should be at the wider end of the teardrop shaped felt. One bar of the bobby pin should be on the top of the felt and the other bar should be on the underside.

7 Layer the velvet leaves on top of the felt and then layer the lace with beads on top of the leaves. Hand-stitch the layers together.

8 Gather your feathers into a bunch so that the ends are aligned. Trim feathers as necessary.

9 While you are still holding the feathers in a bunch with even ends, apply glue to the cut ends to keep the feathers together. Let the glue dry before attaching them. Alternatively, you can wrap the ends of the feathers with floral tape.

10 Insert the glued bunch of feathers between the bottom layer of lace and on top of the velvet leaves.

11 Add additional hand stitches along the bottom of the felt through the lace. Use very small, discrete stitches to secure the piece. Loop a few stitches onto the bobby pin to secure it.

CHAPTER FOUR

Flourishes

USING A MIX OF MATERIALS is an amazing way to create pieces that are both stunning and rich in texture. I am constantly mixing and matching materials to create unique and fresh styles. Finding that perfect vintage lace appliqué or using a fabric in an unexpected way can result in the prettiest surprise.

In this chapter, you will use lace, fabric and beads to create earrings, necklaces, belts, hair adornments and a brooch. These pieces can be worn every day, or you can make them for a specific, special occasion, including a wedding or birthday. When you're searching for materials, don't be afraid to snatch up that pretty ribbon or fancy lace appliqué you've had your eye on. You'll most likely find a perfect use for it, and you'll be able to make a piece that says something about your personal tastes and style.

SOFT PETAL AND APPLIQUÉ NECKLACE

With this style, the flowers can be made in a variety of colors and you may choose the beaded appliqué of your choice. There are two handmade flowers that utilize two different methods to achieve a similar result. You can practice both methods and use the style you most prefer. This piece can be made with more of a curve if you'd like to wear it closer to your neck, or straighter, which would allow you to also wear it as a belt.

MATERIALS

15" × 24" (38cm × 61cm) piece of silk chiffon or soft, thin fabric

6" × 32" (15cm × 81cm) piece of silk or soft fabric

16" (40.5cm) of ½"–1" (1cm–2.5cm) wide ribbon

2 small appliqués, 1"–3" (2.5cm–7.5cm) long

2" × 6" (5cm × 15cm) of felt or interfacing, cut into a long crescent

4–6 velvet leaves

TOOLS

needle

thread

scissors

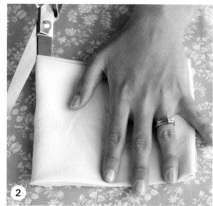

1 Fold the 15" × 24" (38cm × 61cm) piece of fabric lengthwise into thirds so the fabric becomes 24" (61cm) long by 5" (12.5cm) wide, with three layers. Fold the fabric in half width-wise, and then in half widthwise again.

2 Using larger scissors, cut the thick fold so you have two piles of folded fabric squares.

3 Repeat Step 2 with each pile by cutting the folds to create more squares of fabric. Doing this will make cutting petals easier by reducing the thickness of fabric.

4 You now have four piles of cut squares. Fold one pile in half, then in half again to create a smaller folded square.

5 Fold the square on the diagonal, along the folded edge and not the cut edge, bringing opposite corners together.

6 Use a larger pair of scissors to cut a triangle point out of the cut end of folded fabric. You can easily do this by cutting two separate straight cuts that are parallel to the opposite folded end. Repeat Steps 4–6 with the remaining piles of square fabric. You may have extra petals. You can save them for another project or add them to the current flower to make it fuller.

7 After cutting the petals, open the fabric and inspect the flowers you have created. Trim any rough edges if necessary.

8 Stack three to six layers of petals and bunch them together on the underside.

9 Hand-stitch the bunched area together tightly. Repeat Step 8, but this time, do not bunch the petals as tightly.

10 Place the more tightly stitched petal bunch on top of the loose petal bunch to create a flower.

11 Flip the bunches over and stitch them together tightly.

12 Flip the flower over and inspect it. You may want to add additional stitches on the back side to create a tighter flower if needed.

13 Fold the 36" × 6" (91.5cm × 15cm) strip of silk in half widthwise about five times or until it measures about 1" × 6" (2.5cm × 15cm).

14 Using large scissors, cut a rounded petal on one end of the cut edge of fabric. Make sure to cut through all the layers.

15 After the petals are cut, open the fabric and inspect the petals. Trim any jagged edges if necessary.

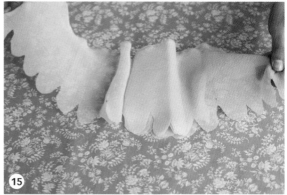

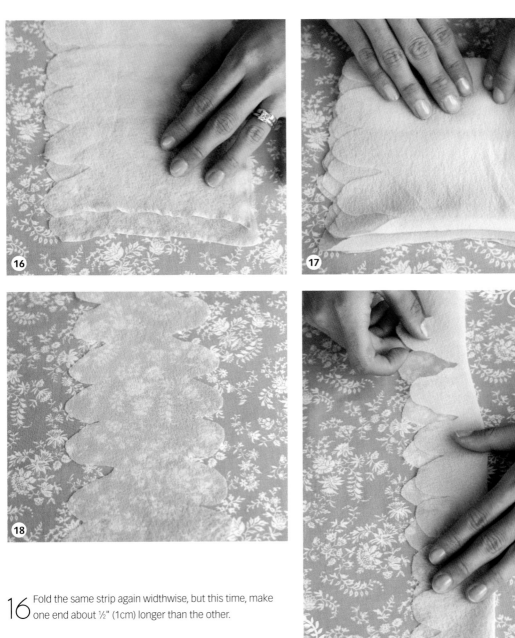

16 Fold the same strip again widthwise, but this time, make one end about ½" (1cm) longer than the other.

17 Fold the fabric in half widthwise until it is about 1" (2.5cm) wide. Cut a rounded petal in the opposite cut end.

18 After opening the fabric again, inspect the petals and round any rough spots as needed.

19 Fold the fabric in half lengthwise. The petals should not sit directly on top of each other but should be staggered.

20 Starting at one end of the folded petal strip, bunch a few petals together, working in a circular direction.

21 Stitch the bunched end together at the folded edge.

22 Keep wrapping a few petals around the growing blossom, stitching as you wrap. You can vary the amount of petals and how tightly you stitch to create a more organic form.

23 Cut the 16" (40.5cm) ribbon in half and stitch a ribbon to each end of the crescent-shaped felt.

24 Place the velvet leaves on the ends of the felt above the ribbon in a pleasing arrangement. If the velvet leaves have attached wire, you can either remove it or twist the wires together tightly in a circle. Stich the velvet leaves into place.

25 Place the appliqués so they cover the velvet leaves slightly. Arrange as desired and stitch them into place.

26 Place the two silk flowers on the piece to determine overall balance and placement. You may need to trim the felt if any is showing on the topside.

27 Hand-stitch the flowers onto the felt by stitching along the bunched underside of each flower until all are securely attached. Trim any thread ends to finish.

LACE POUF
BLOSSOM BROOCH

Sweet poufs of lace cannot be beat! This design can be made in a variety of sizes and in any number you choose. You could create two or three different sizes and wear them bunched together on a jacket, or create a pair and use them as shoe clips. If you'd prefer, you can even attach a comb or clip to the back and wear one in your hair. This piece can also be made with fabric if you don't want to use lace, and it requires just simple hand-cutting and sewing to complete.

MATERIALS

1 brooch pin

(5) 3" (7.5cm) squares of soft lace

TOOLS

thread

scissors

needle

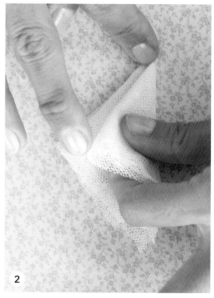

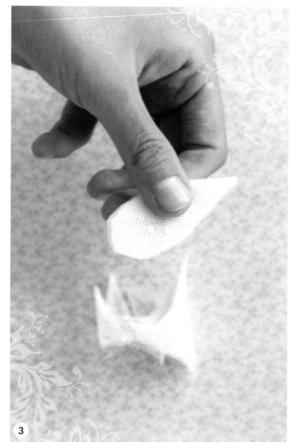

1 Stack two squares of fabric and fold them in half, then in half again, resulting in a square of folded fabric.

2 Fold the fabric on the diagonal.

3 Using a larger pair of scissors, cut a rounded petal through all the layers on the cut end of the folded fabric.

4 Open the lace flower layer and inspect the petals. Trim any rough edges if necessary. Repeat Steps 1–4 for the remaining pieces of square lace.

5 Layer the petals on top of each other. Stagger them slightly so they don't lay directly on top of each other. This will help create a prettier and fuller flower.

6 Bunch the center of all petal layers together at the bottom and hand-stitch through all the layers to join. You can bunch and stitch through several times to create a secure and full bloom.

7 Hand-stitch a brooch pin to the back of the piece. Use several stitches to make sure it is secure.

DOUBLE-FINISHED LACE FLOWER NECKLACE

Flowers are such a lovely accessory to wear, and this design showcases them front and center. This necklace is shown in earthy, natural tones, which are wonderful for everyday wear. You can make it more glamorous by using different fabrics and colors or by using more rhinestones or crystals. This piece could also be worn as a belt or headband. It is mostly created with hand-sewing techniques, which makes it a perfect evening or weekend project.

MATERIALS

18" (45.5cm) square of lace

18" (45.5cm) square of silk organza or sheer fabric

1 crescent-shaped piece of felt, approximately 5" (12.5cm) long

7–10 assorted beads, pearls or crystals

1 flower appliqué

30" (76cm) of ¾" (2cm) wide ribbon

3 velvet leaves

TOOLS

needle

thread

scissors

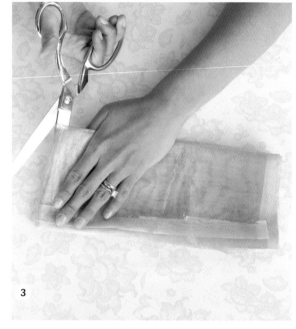

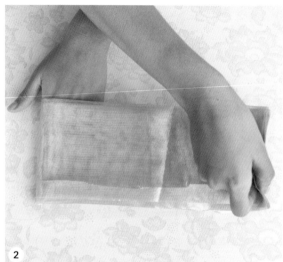

1 Fold the fabric lengthwise into four equal parts. Folding will help create even petals and will speed the cutting process by reducing repetition.

2 Fold the fabric in half widthwise.

3 Slide the scissors into the fold and cut to create two pieces of folded fabric.

4 Fold each portion of fabric in half again to create rough squares.

5 Make a rounded cut in the folded fabric. Make sure you cut the open end of the fabric, keeping the folded corner closer to you.

6 Repeat Steps 4–5 with the second portion of fabric.

7 Separate the pieces and inspect the petals.

8 Tie thread to one end of a folded-over petal piece and stitch along the open edges to close and gather them.

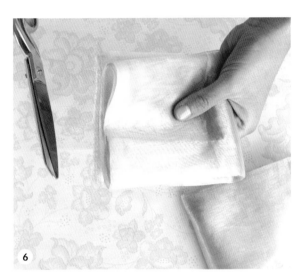

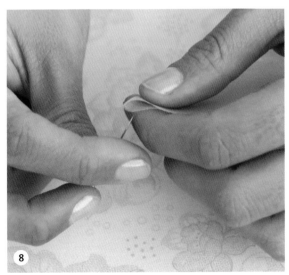

9 You can tie off and cut the thread, or you can leave it on the needle and add another petal, repeating Step 8.

10 Keep gathering petals and adding to the flower until it has five petals.

11 When the flower is finished, hand-sew several beads to the center of the flower.

12 Repeat Steps 1–12 with the lace fabric.

13

14

15

16

13 Join the leaves together in bunches of two or three by twisting the wires together. If your leaves do not have wires, you can hand-sew them together.

14 Hand-stitch one velvet leaf bunch to one end of the crescent-shaped felt.

15 Sew the lace flower onto the felt next to the velvet leaves. Sew the fabric flower next to the lace flower.

16 Hand-sew the small lace appliqué to the end of the felt. Cut the 30" (76cm) ribbon in half and sew one half to the end of the piece, between the felt and appliqué. Repeat with the other half of the ribbon, stitching it between the felt and velvet leaves.

CREAMY LACE BELT

This sweet and light belt is simple in its construction but dramatic in its overall result. You can use an assortment of laces in various sizes. I like to use a larger lace for the base and small pieces of lace that were left over from other projects for layering. Feel free to use vintage and new lace and add buttons, beads or other embellishments of your choice. This piece is constructed with simple hand-sewing techniques.

MATERIALS

60"–75" (152.5cm–190.5cm) of ½"–1" (13mm–2.5cm) wide ribbon

5–8 pieces of assorted lace

20–30 assorted loose beads, pearls or rhinestones

2 pieces of tulle, about 8" × 3" (20.5cm × 7.5cm), cut into an elongated oval shape

TOOLS

needle

thread

scissors

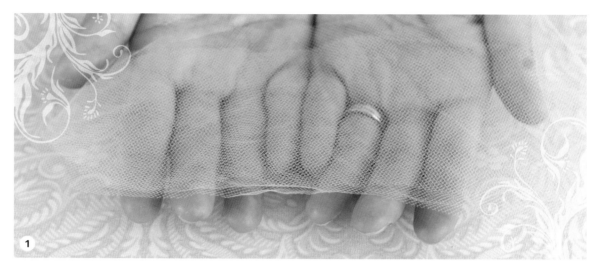

1 Two elongated ovals of tulle, layered on top of one another, will serve as the base or foundation for the belt.

2 Place the lace pieces on the tulle and arrange them to cover most of the tulle. You don't have to cover all of the tulle. Small, visible sections of tulle add to the ethereal look of the piece.

3 You may want to slip some pieces of lace partially underneath other pieces. Layering multiple types of lace will give the piece a decadent look.

4

5

4 Pin the pieces down if you'd like, and carefully begin stitching the lace onto the tulle.

5 Hand-sew beads on top of the lace. You can sew beads in clusters and spread them out as well.

6 After all the beads are sewn on, turn the belt over and center the ribbon over the tulle. Hand-sew the ribbon onto the tulle.

6

LACE AND LEAF HEADBAND

This vintage-inspired piece would be a perfect project for a do-it-yourself bride. It is easy to wear and would be a wonderful way to complete a wedding day look. This piece will look different depending on the lace and leaves you use. You could also adapt the piece for different occasions by simply switching the colors. For instance, if you used silver or icy blue, it would be a great holiday party headband. This project requires simple hand-sewing skills, and the end result is breathtaking.

MATERIALS

7–8 small velvet leaves

1–3 large velvet leaves

1 satin-covered headband

(2) 3" × 6" (7.5cm × 15cm) pieces of tulle

2–3 medium-sized lace appliqués

1 piece of felt, approximately 3"–4" (7.5cm–10cm) long × 1" (2.5cm) wide

TOOLS

scissors

needle

thread

fabric glue

1 If the smaller leaves you are using are already wired together, shape them along the band of the headband and wrap the wire onto the band. Add additional hand stitches as needed to secure. If your leaves are not wired, hand-stitch them individually to the headband.

2 Place the larger velvet leaves on the headband on top of the smaller leaves and hand-sew them on. If the velvet leaves have wires, you can wrap them around the band or remove them completely.

3 Position the first lace appliqué over the leaves.

4 Hand sew the lace appliqué onto both the leaves and the headband.

5 Layer the second piece of lace and hand sew it onto the headband. You can overlap it with the first piece of lace if needed. If you have a third appliqué, layer it over the first two.

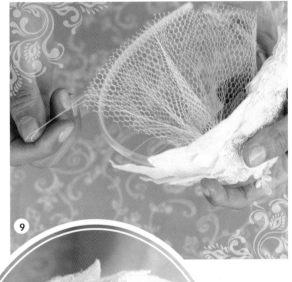

6 Layer the two pieces of tulle directly on top of each other.

7 Starting at one end, hand-sew gathers into the long end of the tulle, making sure to go through both pieces of tulle. Use stitches about ½" (1cm) long. To sew gathers, sew a straight stitch about ¼" (6mm) from the edge of the fabric. Pull the thread at the end to bunch and gather the fabric.

8 When you have reached one end, pull the thread to gather the tulle and tie it off. It should resemble a small fan.

9 Hand-sew the tulle fan to the underside of the leaves and headband, about one-third of the way up the headband. Secure the thread and trim to finish.

SILVER ROSETTE MINI HAT

If you're in need of a festive hair accessory, this mini hat is the perfect piece. It has a vintage feel and, due to its mini size, isn't overpowering. You can use an assortment of beads on this piece, and, if you like, you can even attach vintage buttons, brooches or lace to make it truly personal. This project will teach you a simple way to create fabric rosettes that can be used for a variety of other accessories.

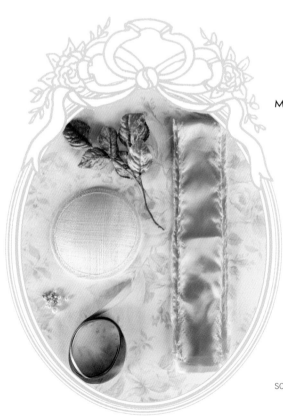

MATERIALS

(1) 5" (12.5cm) buckram or sinamay circle frame

6 velvet millinery leaves, twisted together in a group of 2 and a group of 4

(2) 12" (30.5cm) pieces of ½" (1cm) wide ribbon, cut into 2 equal pieces

(8) 3mm round beads

1–3 large round beads

assorted rhinestones or crystal beads

(2) 1½" × 15" (4cm × 38cm) strips of polyester, silk or cotton fabric

TOOLS

needle

thread

scissors

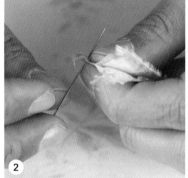

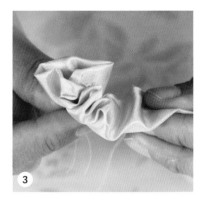

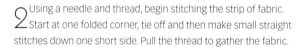

1 Fold one 1½" × 15" (4cm × 38cm) strip of fabric in half lengthwise.

2 Using a needle and thread, begin stitching the strip of fabric. Start at one folded corner, tie off and then make small straight stitches down one short side. Pull the thread to gather the fabric.

3 To create the mini rose, begin wrapping the folded fabric around itself in a circular pattern. With every half- to full-wrap, add stitches to the cut end to secure.

4 Wrap the fabric around the forming flower and continue to stitch as you go. When you have reached the end of the fabric, tie off. Repeat Steps 3–4 with the second strip of fabric to make two rosettes.

5 Position the flowers and leaves on the buckram frame. This will help you arrange the elements in a way that is the most pleasing to you.

6 Start sewing on the individual pieces. It is easier to sew the leaves on first and then the rosettes so you can cover the twisted wires of the leaves if necessary.

7 After you have sewn on a rosette, sew pearl beads and crystals into the center of it. Repeat with the remaining rosette.

8 Fold in the end of one 12" (30.5cm) piece of ribbon about ¼" (6mm), then fold it in again. This will create a cleaner finish and prevent fraying.

9 Turn the frame over so the underside is facing you. Starting at the edge of the frame, about a half to three-fourths of the way back, sew on the folded end of the ribbon. Repeat Steps 8–9 for the second ribbon, sewing the ribbon on the opposite side.

10 Hand-sew the crystals and beads onto the top of the frame. They can be in a random pattern or more clustered. Sew from the underside to the topside to conceal the thread. Tie off and trim the threads to finish.

SILK BLOSSOM DANGLE EARRINGS

These beautiful floral earrings are reminiscent of a lotus or lily flower with their stamens and petals. They are definitely attention-getting statement earrings. You can use a variety of beads for these earrings, and you'll utilize simple wire-wrapping skills when creating them.

MATERIALS

(2) 3" × 6" (7.5cm × 15cm) pieces of silk or other fabric, starched

(2) 3mm jump rings

2 small floral bead caps

2 hook ear wires

6 freshwater pearls or other small beads, approximately 4mm

2 drop crystals, approximately 4mm–6mm long

2½" × 2½" (6.5cm × 6.5cm) chain, 2 each of the following lengths: 3½" (9cm), 2¼" (6cm), 2" (5cm), 1½" (4cm) and ¾" (2cm)

(8) 1½" (4cm) pieces of 28-gauge wire

(2) 26- to 28-gauge brass eye pins, 1"–2" (2.5cm–5cm) long

TOOLS

wire cutters

scissors

needle

thread

round-nose pliers

half-round pliers

1 Make widthwise accordion folds about 8mm apart in the entirety of the silk fabric.

2 Cut a rounded petal on one short end of the folded fabric. It will look like a rounded-edge fan when finished. Repeat Steps 1–2 for the second piece of fabric.

3 Feed a 1½" (4cm) piece of 28-gauge wire through a 4mm pearl bead, centering it on the bead.

4 Choose one of the cut chains, but not the longest length (3½" [9cm]) or the shortest (¾" [2cm]). Insert the wire with the pearl through the last link of the chain.

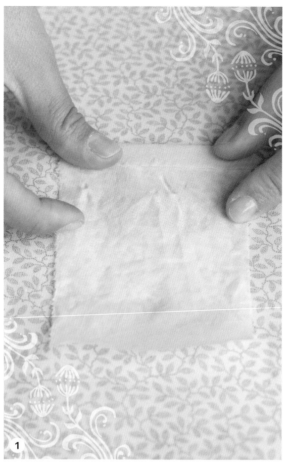

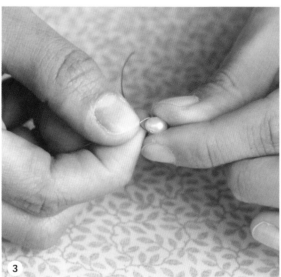

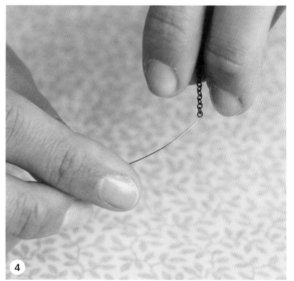

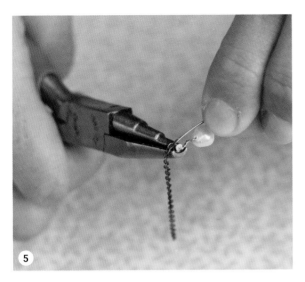

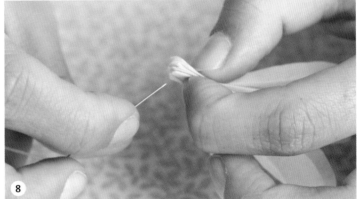

5 Using the half-round pliers, grip the wire about ¼" (6mm) away from the pearl bead. Keeping the wire in the pliers, pull one end of the wire over the top of the pliers.

6 Twist the wire around itself three to four times. Trim the excess wire and tuck in the end. Repeat Steps 3–6 for all the remaining pearls. Repeat these steps with the 3½" (9cm) chains, using the drop crystals instead of the pearls.

7 Slip an eye pin through the ends of three of the chains with pearls (one chain of each length) and one chain with a drop crystal. Repeat with the other eye pin and the remaining chains with pearls and chain with a drop crystal. Set aside.

8 Pinch the flat end of the fabric petal fan and sew the folds together so it looks like a burst of petals.

9

10

11

9 Feed the end of one of the eye pin components made in Step 7 through the middle pleat of the petal fan. There should be a gap between the stitches, and you may need to wiggle the eye pin a bit to get it through. Pull the eye pin mostly through so the chains are tucked between the folds of the petals.

10 Next, stitch the folds on either side of the chains together with a few stitches. This will allow the chains and petals to hang straight down.

11 Slip a floral bead cap onto the end of the eye pin, with the petals facing down. Slide the bead cap until the silk fabric is tucked into it.

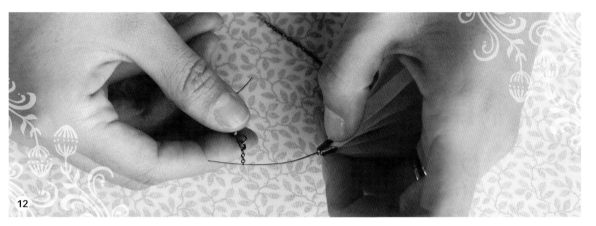

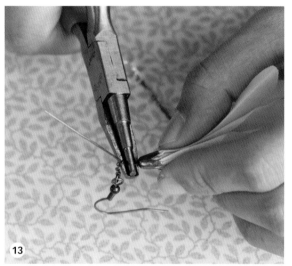

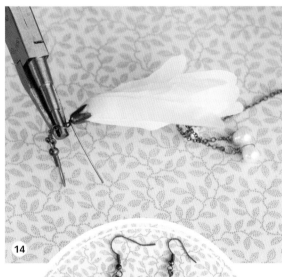

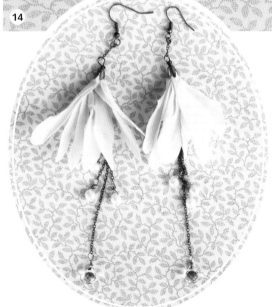

12 Attach the ¾" (2cm) chain to a jump ring and the jump ring to an ear wire. Close the jump ring. Insert the end of the eye pin through the last link of the ¾" (2cm) chain.

13 Grip the eye pin with the half-round pliers close to the bead cap.

14 Now twist the wire over the top of the pliers and twist it around itself two to three times. Trim the excess wire and tuck in the ends to finish. Repeat Steps 8–14 to complete the second earring.

DUSTY GREEN AND GRAY SILK FLOWER AND LACE BELT

Adorn your waistline with an amazing burst of flowers and lace that will add a beautiful element of interest to any dress. This gorgeous and texturally-rich piece is easy to wear and could also be worn as a dramatic headband. It uses millinery-pressing and hand-sewing techniques. You can customize with your own choice of colors and lace.

MATERIALS

2 faux dusty miller fabric leaves

2–3 assorted lace appliqués

(4) 3½" (9cm) squares of satin or other smooth fabric

5 circles of cotton linen fabric measuring 5" (12.5cm), 4¾" (12cm), 4½" (11.5cm), 4¼" (11cm) and 4" (10cm) across

40" (101.5cm) of ribbon (longer or shorter as needed)

3–5 assorted round beads, approximately 4mm–6mm

1 elongated oval-shaped piece of felt or interfacing, approximately 3" × 7" (7.5cm × 18cm)

TOOLS

scissors

millinery irons or dapping set

foam pad covered with cotton fabric

needle

thread

1 Cut the fabric circles into five-point petal layers. Make the bottom layer about 4"–5" (10cm–12.5cm) across and each subsequent layer about [½" (1cm) smaller]. When finished, you should have five different sizes.

2 Using a larger millinery iron or dapping tool, press all the petal points (see *Shaping and Pressing Petals* on page 21).

3 Place two dusty miller leaves on one end of the felt. Layer one of the lace appliqués over the leaves.

4 Continue layering appliqués and silk flowers onto the belt. After placing all the elements onto the felt, set the entire piece aside. Layering them now will help determine the final placement.

1

2

3

4

5

6

7

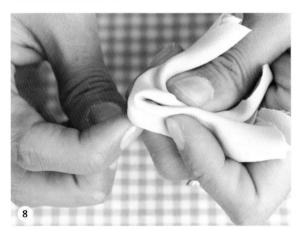

8

5   Hand-sew the lace and leaves onto the felt.

6   Cut five-point petal layers from four 3½" (9cm) satin squares. These can be roughly the same size.

7   Place the satin petals on top of each other so the petals are staggered and do not sit directly on top of the previous layer.

8   Turn the fabric over, making sure to hold the layers in place, and bunch the centers together.

9 Stitch the gathered portion of fabric together to create the fluffy shape of the flower.

10 Position both handmade flowers on the felt toward the center of the design. If you'd like, you can use pins to keep the elements in place.

11 Remove the satin flower while you sew the pressed flower onto the belt to make sewing easier.

12 Hand-sew several pearl beads and crystals into the center of the pressed flower.

13 Place the satin flower close to the pressed flower or even slightly underneath it. Hand-sew it in place and tie off on the back side.

14 Center the ribbon on the back of the felt and hand-sew it to the piece.

RESOURCES

THE BULK OF THE tools and materials used in this book can be found at your local craft or fabric store. There are some items that are a little harder to source and I've listed options here, along with some favorite places to find items used in this book.

Hats by Leko
www.hatsupply.com
buckram hat frames, silk millinery flowers, velvet millinery leaves, stamens and veiling

Etsy
www.etsy.com
jewelry findings, new and vintage millinery flowers, velvet millinery leaves, sinamay frames

Fire Mountain Gems and Beads
www.firemountaingems.com
jump rings, pliers, wire and clasps

Plumes N' Feathers
www.plumesnfeathers.com
feathers

Lacis
www.lacis.com/catalog
millinery irons; search for "flower iron"

M & J Trimming
www.mjtrim.com
ribbons

Torb and Reiner
www.torbandreiner.com/online-shop-1/
millinery-tools
millinery irons with wooden handles

INDEX

adhesives, 13
alligator clips. See hair clips
appliqué needles, 18
appliqués. See lace appliqués

backing, felt, 12, 24, 47, 51, 67, 79
beads, 10, 63, 94, 114, 119, 127.
    See also pearls
    pearl beads, 130–131, 139
    seed beads, 10
    wire wrapping, 25
belts, 12
    Creamy Lace Belt, 116–119
    Dusty Green and Gray Silk Flower
    and Lace Belt, 134–139
bobby pins, 14
    Lace Embellished Bobby Pin, 92–95
brooches
    Feather Spray Brooch, 70–73
    Lace Pouf Blossom Brooch,
    106–109
buckram frame, 124–127

chain, 14
    brass, 80–85
clips. See alligator clips; hair clips
combs, 14, 24, 48–51, 64–67
    Blossom and Pearl Comb, 52–57
    Blushing Silk Petals Hair Comb,
    36–41
    Oversized Handmade Silk Flower
    Comb, 64–67
    Petite Silk Cluster Flower Comb,
    48–51
corsages
    Golden Floral Wrist Corsage, 30–35
crystals, 10, 60–61, 63, 94, 127, 139

dapping tools, 17, 32. See also millinery
    flower irons

earrings
    Silk Blossom Dangle Earrings,
    128–133
    Soft Feather Dangle Earrings,
    80–85
epoxy glue, 13

fabric, 12. See also felt; lace
    cotton, 12, 30–35, 54, 60, 66,
    76–77, 124–127
    cotton linen, 12, 134–136
    cotton voile, 12

lace, 13, 73, 94–95, 106–109, 118
    patterned silk, 42–47
    polyester, 124–127
    satin, 134–137
    silk, 12, 50, 54, 60, 66, 76–77,
    100–105, 124–133
    silk chiffon, 12, 36–41, 100–105
    silk habotai, 12, 36–41
    starching, 20
    tulle, 118–119, 122–123
fabric flowers, 10
fabric glue, 13
fabric stiffeners, 13, 20
feathers, 11, 68–95
    duck, 11, 86–89
    goose, 11, 74, 77, 80–83, 86–89
    guinea hen, 11, 80–83
    ostrich, 11, 86–89, 92–95
    peacock, 11, 86–89
    pheasant, 11
    rooster, 11, 80–83, 92–95
felt, 12. See also backing, felt
findings, 14
flourishes, 96–139
flower irons, millinery. See millinery
    flower irons
flowers, 29–67
    fabric, 10
    pressed, 12–13, 21
    silk, 10, 51, 105
    stitched, 100–105, 108–109,
    112–115, 137–138
foam rubber pad, covered, 18, 21

glue, 13

hair clips, 14, 79
    Feather and Burnt Silk Petal Hair
    Clip, 74–79

hats
    Silver Rosette Mini Hat, 124–127
headbands, 14, 24
    Lace and Leaf Headband, 120–123
    Patterned Silk Flower Headband,
    42–47

interfacing, 12

jewelry-making tools, 19
jump rings, 24, 80–85, 90–91, 133

lace, 13, 73, 94–95, 105–109, 118. See
    also fabric, lace; lace appliqués
    cutting appliqués from, 22
lingerie, 12
lace appliqués, 13, 22, 77, 94–95, 115,

122–123, 134–137
leaves, 11
    dusty miller, 11, 134–139
    millinery, 124–127
    silk, 51
    velvet, 11, 34, 46, 51, 67, 92–95,
    105, 115, 120–123
    vintage, 11
loops, creating, 26

materials, 10–14
millinery flower irons, 17, 21. See also
    petals, shaping and pressing

necklaces
    Blossom and Pearl Necklace, 58–63
    Double-Finished Lace Flower
    Necklace, 110–115
    Pink Curved Feather Necklace,
    86–91
    Soft Petal and Appliqué Necklace,
    98–105
needles, sewing, 18

pearls, 10, 54–57, 63. See also beads
petals
    curling, 66
    cutting freehand, 27, 32, 38–39, 44,
    60, 66, 76, 100–103, 108, 130, 136
    shaping and pressing, 21, 33, 39,
    50, 54, 60, 136
pliers, 19, 24, 26

ribbons, 12
rosettes, creating, 126–127

scissors, 18–19
sewing needles, 18
    128–133
silk flowers, 10, 51, 105
sinamay frame, 124–127
singeing silk, 76
stabilizer, 12
stamen clusters, 34–35, 46, 66–67
    making, 23
stamens, 11, 23
starches, 13, 20

techniques, 20–27
thread, 18
tools, 16–19

wire, 14
    brass, 80–85
wire cutters, 19
wire wrapping, 19, 25–26
wrist corsage, 30–35

ABOUT THE AUTHOR

MYRA CALLAN RECEIVED a master of arts degree in geography from the University of California, Davis. Her love for science and the environment is expressed through her designs, which are all experiments of color, form and texture. Myra is completely self-taught and is the owner and designer of Twigs & Honey, which began in 2008. Her work has been featured on the *TODAY* show and in *Us Weekly* magazine, *BRIDES* magazine, *Bridal Guide* magazine, *Real Simple* magazine, *The Los Angeles Times* and countless other publications. She has also designed and created pieces for the nationwide store windows of Ann Taylor and has designed exclusive pieces for BHLDN. She carries her Twigs & Honey line through boutiques and online through her website and Etsy shop. Myra lives in Oregon with her husband, Matt, Siberian husky, Indy, and parakeet, Kiwi.

www.fwmedia.com

16 15 14 13 12   5 4 3 2 1

Distributed in Canada by Fraser Direct
100 Armstrong Avenue
Georgetown, ON, Canada L7G 5S4
Tel: (905) 877-4411

Distributed in the U.K. and Europe by F&W MEDIA INTERNATIONAL
Brunel House, Newton Abbot, Devon, TQ12 4PU, England
Tel: (+44) 1626 323200, Fax: (+44) 1626 323319
Email: enquiries@fwmedia.com
Distributed in Australia by Capricorn Link
P.O. Box 704, S. Windsor NSW, 2756 Australia
Tel: (02) 4577-3555

SRN: W7141
ISBN-13: 978-1-4402-2934-3

Editor: Rachel Scheller
Designer: Prudence Rogers
Photographer: Elizabeth Messina
Production Coordinator: Greg Nock

Metric Conversion Chart

To convert	to	multiply by
Inches	Centimeters	2.54
Centimeters	Inches	0.4
Feet	Centimeters	30.5
Centimeters	Feet	0.03
Yards	Meters	0.9
Meters	Yards	1.1

ACKNOWLEDGMENTS

I feel very grateful to everyone who contributed to my first book, whether with their time, talent, product or support. I thank you tremendously.

I would first like to thank the amazing photographer and my good friend, Elizabeth Messina. Elizabeth has been a wonderful supporter of both Twigs & Honey and me. Her kindness and generosity never cease to amaze me. I've had the privilege of working with her on numerous projects and photo shoots, and her talent and professionalism are second to none. Through her photography, Elizabeth is able to capture life, love, happiness and everything in between with grace and ease, and her photos are truly works of art.

I would like to thank all the amazing individuals that contributed to the success of our photo shoots. Thank you to our beautiful models: Dominique Farias, Kate Towers, Lavenda Memory, Meredith Adelaide, Amy Stewart and Mikaela, who were all so sweet and patient during the long shoots. You ladies were wonderful. Many thanks goes to Madeline Roosevelt for her unwavering sweetness and amazing makeup and hair artistry. Thank you to Jen Alfieri and Abby Auch of the Ace Hotel for allowing us to shoot in the amazing event space, The Cleaners, in Portland, Oregon. I would also like to thank Jessica Watson Photography for allowing us to shoot in her lovely Æther Studio and for helping with numerous errands throughout the shoot. I would like to extend a very warm thank you to our assistant during the shoot, Rebekah Shaddy, who helped with note taking, set-up, ironing, cleaning up and so much more than was expected of her. Gratitude goes to designers Holly Stalder, Kate Towers and Ivy & Aster for kindly allowing us to use your beautiful creations for the wardrobe. Also, special thanks to Lanie List, owner of Lovely Bridal Shop, for letting us borrow beautiful dresses from your shop all the way on the opposite coast. Thank you to Joy Deangdeelert Cho of Oh Joy! for your pretty wallpaper designs, and to Christiana and Aimee of Hygge & West for being so generous and sending Oh Joy! wallpaper for us to use in our backdrops.

I would also like to specially thank all the supporters, fans, blog readers and Twigs & Honey clients who have helped me do what I love. I also thank the publications, bloggers and industry professionals who have helped spread the word on Twigs & Honey and are also valuable sources of daily inspiration.

A wonderful thank you to our supporters at F+W Media and North Light Craft: Editor Vanessa Lyman, who first "found" me and helped the book get off the ground with her kindness and confidence; editor Rachel Scheller for her expertise, knowledge and guidance; and our designer Prudence Rogers, for her talent and experience with executing a vision.

Of course, I must also thank my wonderful husband, Matt, who was not only a cheerleader and emotional support, but who helped with all the heavy lifting, literally. From helping construct the wooden wallpaper backdrops to hauling a vintage sewing table, I could not have completed this book without his thoughtfulness, help and love.

DISCOVER MORE WAYS
TO ADORN YOURSELF

BEADED ALLURE
by Kelly Wiese

Add a romantic twist to your creative time with *Beaded Allure*. Inside you'll find projects and techniques to give your beadweaving the soft and romantic aesthetic you've always dreamed of. Author Kelly Wiese will lead you through the ins and outs of a variety of stitches, and you'll use those stitches in 25 step-by-step projects.

HEADS UP
by Carol Meldrum

Fascinators, headbands and hair clips of every shape and size are more popular than ever. This collection of eyecatching projects shows you how easily you can create your own unique, quirky and colorful hair accessories.

For inspiring books like these, plus the fabric, tools and notions you'll need, visit store.marthapullen.com.